Beginner's Guide to SolidWorks 2013 – Level I

Alejandro Reyes, MSME
Certified SolidWorks Professional

ISBN: 978-1-58503-774-2

SDC
Publications

Schroff Development Corporation

www.SDCpublications.com

Schroff Development Corporation

P.O. Box 1334

Mission KS 66222

(913) 262-2664

www.SDCpublications.com

Publisher: Stephen Schroff

Trademarks and Disclaimer

SolidWorks and its family of products are registered trademarks of Dassault Systemes. Microsoft Windows and its family products are registered trademarks of the Microsoft Corporation.

Every effort has been made to provide an accurate text. The author and the manufacturers shall not be held liable for any parts developed with this book or held responsible for any inaccuracies or errors that appear in the book.

Examination Copies:

Books received as examination copies are for review purposes only and may not be made available for student use. Resale of examination copies is prohibited.

Electronic Files:

Any electronic files associated with this book are licensed to the original user only. These files may not be transferred to any other party.

Acknowledgements

Beginner's Guide to SolidWorks is dedicated to my lovely wife Patricia and my kids Liz, Ale and Hector, all of whom have always been very supportive, patient and comprehensive during the writing of this book. To you, all my love.

Also, I wish to thank the hundreds of students, users, teachers and engineers whose great ideas and words of encouragement have helped me improve this book and make it a great success.

About the Author

Alejandro Reyes holds a BSME from the Instituto Tecnológico de Ciudad Juárez, Mexico in electro-mechanical engineering and a Masters Degree from the University of Texas at El Paso in mechanical design, with strong focus in Materials Science and Finite Element Analysis.

Alejandro spent more than 8 years as a SolidWorks Value Added Reseller. During this time he was a Certified SolidWorks Instructor and Support Technician, CosmosWorks Support Technician, and a Certified SolidWorks Professional, credential that he still maintains. Alejandro has over 19 years of experience using CAD/CAM/FEA software and is currently the President of MechaniCAD Inc.

His professional interests include finding alternatives and improvements to existing products, FEA analysis and new technologies. On a personal level, he enjoys bicycle riding and spending time with family and friends.

Notes:

Table of Contents

List of commands introduced in each chapter. Note that many commands are used extensively in following chapters after been presented.

PART MODELING

Housing:
New Part
Create Sketch
Confirmation Corner
Sketch Grid
Auto-Rotate view normal to Sketch plane
Sketch Rectangle
Sketch Centerline
Sketch Relations
Smart Dimension
Sketch Status
Extrude Boss/Base
Document Units
View Orientation
Mouse Gestures
Menu Customization
Center Rectangle
Fillet
Magnifying Glass
Extruded Cut
Through All (End condition)
Sketch Fillet
Rename Features
Circle
Instant 3D
Mirror Features
Model Display Styles
Fly-Out FeatureManager
Dimension Tolerance
Hole Wizard
Cosmetic Threads
Sketch Point
Edit Sketch
Rebuild
Circular Pattern
Automatic Relations
Temporary Axes

Sketch Slot
Sketch Numeric Input
Linear Pattern
Edit Material
Mass Properties

Side Cover
Revolved Boss/Base
Trim Entities
Extend Entities
Construction Geometry

Top Cover
Offset Entities
Mirror Entities (Sketch)
Up to Surface (End condition)
Shell
Measure Tool
Select Other
More Fillet options

Offset Shaft
Revolved Cut
Auxiliary Planes
Hide/Show sketch
Convert Entities
Polygon (Sketch)
Flip Side to Cut
Axis (Reference geometry)
Coordinate Systems

Worm Gear
Mid Plane (End Condition)
Chamfer
Dimension to Arc
Direction 2 (End Condition)

Worm Gear Shaft
General Review of previous commands

SWEEP, LOFT, WRAP

Sweep
Thin Feature
Ellipse
Auxiliary Plane at point
Sweep
Up to Next (End condition)
Full Round Fillet
Helix
Variable pitch helix
Open Sketch Cut
Guide Curves

Loft
Offset Plane
Hide/Show Plane
Loft
Start/End Conditions
Model Section View

Wrap
Wrap
Intersection Curve

DETAIL DRAWING

Housing Drawing
Part Configurations
Suppress Feature
Parent Child Relation
Unsuppress
Configure Dimensions
Change Configuration
New Drawing
Make Drawing from Part
View Palette (Drawing)
Projected View
Tangent Edge Display
Section View
Detail View
Model Items
(Import dimensions)

Drawing cleanup
Center Mark/Centerlines
Add Sheet to Drawing
Model View
   Configuration
Rename Sheet
Layers

Side Cover Drawing
Reference Dimension
Dimension Parentheses
Sheet Scale
View Scale

Top Cover Drawing
Display only Cut Surface
Display Dimension As
diameter
Ordinate Dimension
Add to Ordinate
Notes
Custom Document
   Properties
Parametric Notes
Link to Property

Offset Shaft Drawing
Broken View

Worm Gear Drawing
Display Sheet Format
Insert Model View
Crop View
Ellipse
Angle Dimension
Tolerance/Precision
Chamfer Dimension
Edit Sheet Format / Title
   Block
Edit Sheet

**Worm Gear Shaft
Drawing**
Broken-Out Section
Spline

ASSEMBLY MODELING

New Assembly
Add New Component
Change Configuration
Mates
Concentric Mate
Coincident Mate
Move Component
Rotate Component
Change Appearance
Parallel Mate
Hide/Show Component
SmartMates
Mirror Components
Width Mate
Toolbox Fasteners
Design Library
Add Fasteners
Cosmetic Thread Display
Configurations using
   Design Tables
Show Feature
   Dimensions
Rename Dimensions
Edit Design Table
Mate Reference
Design Library
Interference Detection
Change dimensions in
   the assembly
Collision Detection
Isolate
Gear Mate
Component Transparency
Drawing update
Exploded View creation
Collapse View
Animate Exploded view

Assembly Drawing
Show Assembly in
   exploded view
Bill of Materials
Add Custom Properties
   to bill of Materials
Open Part from
   assembly drawing
Format Bill of Materials
Auto Balloons

SimulationXpress
Analysis Background
Split Line
SimulationXpress
Model Fixture
Model Forces
Meshing
Run Simulation
Review results
Factor of Safety
Generate reports
Model changes and
   simulation update
Model optimization

eDrawings

Appendix
Document Templates

In the next book,
Beginner's Guide to SolidWorks 2013 <u>Level II</u>
you'll learn:

- Multi body part techniques
- Part editing, equations and errors
- Top Down design techniques
- Design sheet metal parts
- How to build and use Libraries
- 3D Sketches
- Design welded structures
- Structural member libraries
- Surface modeling
- Mold design tools
- And more…

Introduction

This book is intended to help new users to learn the basic concepts of SolidWorks and good solid modeling techniques in an easy to follow guide. It will be a great starting point for those new to SolidWorks or as a teaching aid in classroom training to become familiar with the software's interface, basic commands and strategies as the user completes a series of models while learning different ways to accomplish a particular task. At the end of this book, the user will have a good understanding of the SolidWorks interface and the most commonly used commands for part modeling, assembly and detailing after completing a series of components and their 2D drawings complete with Bill of Materials. The book is focused on the processes to complete the modeling of a part, instead of the individual commands or operations, which are learned as we progress. We strived hard to cover the commands required in the **Certified SolidWorks Associate** test as listed in the SolidWorks website as of the writing of this book, and added some more.

SolidWorks is an easy to use yet powerful CAD software that includes many time saving tools that enable new and experienced users to complete design tasks in a very short time. Most commands covered in this book have advanced options, which may or may not be covered in this book. This book is meant to be a starting point to help new users learn the basic and most frequently used commands, and the Level II book covers more advanced and complex commands including sheet metal, mold making, surfacing, etc.

SolidWorks is a leading 3D mainstream design CAD package with hundreds of thousands of users in the industry going from one man shops to Fortune 500 companies, and has a strong presence in the educational market including high schools, vocational schools and many prestigious universities.

We'd love to hear from you, your experience with this book and any other comments or ideas on how we can make it better for you by sending an email to: alejandro@mechanicad.com.

Prerequisites

This book was written assuming the reader has knowledge of the following topics:

- The reader is familiar with the Windows operating system.
- Knowledge of mechanical design and drafting (detailing).
- Any experience with other CAD systems is a plus.
- Understanding of mechanics of materials – a must to understanding SimulationXpress.

Notes:

The SolidWorks Interface

The very first time we open SolidWorks we are presented with the option to select our default drafting standard and units of measure. Selecting a default doesn't mean we have to use those options; we can change either one at any time as we see fit. Most samples and exercises in the book are presented using the ANSI dimensioning standard and inches for units of measure.

The Menu bar is hidden by default. It is automatically displayed when the user moves the pointer over the SolidWorks banner in the upper left corner of the window and is hidden when we move away from it. In order to make the menu bar always visible for ease of clarity in the book, press the pin icon at the end of the menu bar as indicated.

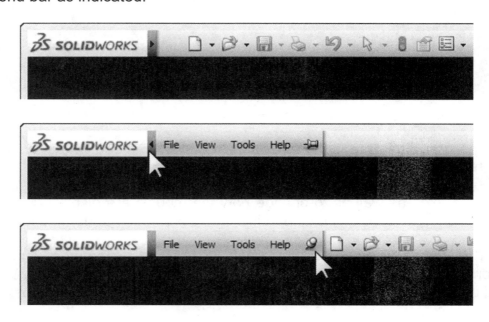

The SolidWorks interface is simple and easy to navigate. The main areas in the interface include toolbars, menus, graphics area, Feature-Manager/PropertyManager and Task Pane. SolidWorks includes an intelligent system of pop up toolbars which is automatically activated when the user selects elements in the FeatureManager or graphics area. SolidWorks has icons and menus similar to those of Microsoft Office applications, and follows Windows rules like drag and drop, copy/paste, etc., typical of any Windows compliant software.

FeatureManager　　**Menus and Toolbars**　　**View Toolbar**　　**Graphics Area**

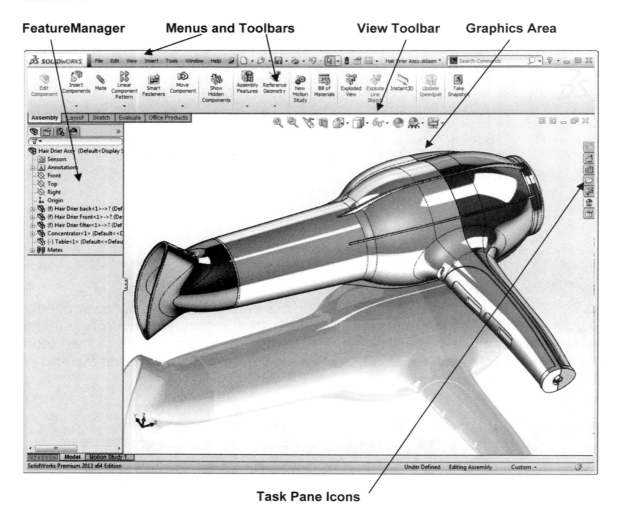

Task Pane Icons

The **graphics area** is the main part of SolidWorks and where most of the action happens; this is where parts, assemblies and drawings are created, visualized and modified. SolidWorks lets users Zoom, Pan, Rotate, change view orientations, etc., as well as to change how the models are displayed, either as Shaded, Hidden Lines, Hidden Lines Visible and Wireframe to name a few.

The **FeatureManager** is the graphical browser of features, operations, parts, drawing views and more which can be edited, modified, deleted, etc. and is located on the left side of the screen.

The FeatureManager's space is also shared by the **PropertyManager** and the **ConfigurationManager**. The PropertyManager is where most of the SolidWorks' command options are presented to the user; this is also where a selected entity's properties are displayed and Configurations are created. The PropertyManager is displayed automatically when needed, so the user does not need to worry about it. We'll show the user how to view both Feature and PropertyManagers at the same time later in the book.

In the PropertyManager we are presented with a consistent, common interface for most commands in SolidWorks, including common controls such as check boxes, open and closed option boxes, action buttons, etc.

To manipulate the models in the graphics area, a set of tools is available from the menu "**View, Modify**" or the right-mouse-button menu in the graphics screen, to Zoom, Pan, Rotate, etc. Select a view manipulation tool, left click-and-drag the mouse in the graphics area to see its effect.

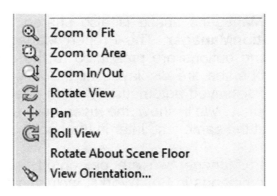

⊕	Zoom to Fit
⊕	Zoom to Area
⊕	Zoom In/Out
⟳	Rotate View
✛	Pan
⟲	Roll View
	Rotate About Scene Floor
✎	View Orientation...

... or using **Mouse Gestures**. Gestures are activated by right-mouse-button-dragging in the graphics area, the gestures shortcuts wheel will appear, and we simply keep dragging to touch the command we want. In order to modify the commands in the wheel we have to select the menu "**Tools, Customize**" and select the Mouse Gestures tab. By default, Mouse Gestures are enabled, but they can be turned off in this tab; we can configure either 4 or 8 gestures for each environment (Part, Assembly, Drawing and Sketch) by selecting the command for each environment from the list of commands and selecting the gesture to assign. In this book we'll use the 8 gesture default settings.

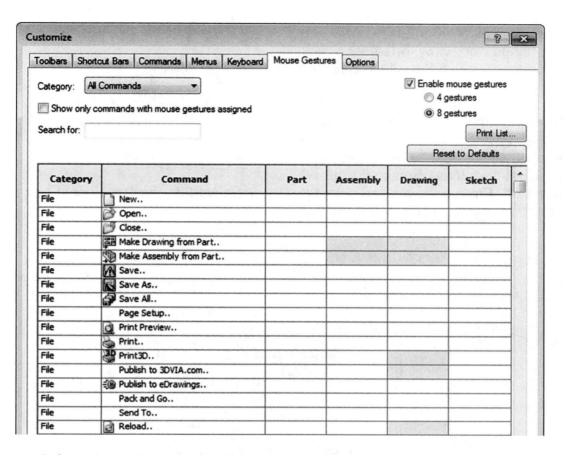

A few shortcuts to manipulate models: The mouse wheel can be used to zoom in and out in the model (the model is zoomed in at the mouse pointer), and clicking the middle mouse button (the wheel) and dragging the mouse **Rotates** the model in the graphics area. The rotation is automatic about the area of the model where the pointer is located. The **Previous View** (default shortcut "Ctrl+Shift+Z") and **Zoom to fit** (default shortcut "F") are single click commands in the view orientation toolbar.

Use the **Standard Views** icon to view the model from any orthogonal view (Front, Back, Left, Bottom, Top, Right, Isometric, etc.). Another way to rotate the models on the screen is with the arrow keys in the keyboard. Holding down the "Shift" key with the arrow keys rotates the model in 90° increments.

In SolidWorks 2013 a new way to change the view orientation was introduced called the View Selector. We can activate it from the "View Orientation" drop down menu or using the shortcut "Ctrl + Spacebar." After activating the View Selector, every time we click in the "View Orientation" we'll get the View Selector until we

turn it off. From here we can select the view we want in the translucent box and the model will be reoriented to that view.

To change the **Display Style** (the way the model looks in the graphics area), the Display Style icon can be selected in the View toolbar; the effects will be immediately visible to the user. Feel free to explore them with your first model to become familiar; sometimes it's convenient to switch to a different view style for visibility or easy selection of internal or hidden entities.

Display Style icon
Shaded with Edges
Shaded
Hidden Lines
Hidden Lines Visible
Wireframe

In this book we will make use of the **CommandManager**. The CommandManager is a tool that consolidates many toolbars in a single location, and selecting a toolbar's tab displays commands available, like Features, Sketch, Detailing, Assembly, Sheet Metal, etc. The CommandManager is a smart feature in SolidWorks – depending on the task at hand, different toolbars will be available to the user – and is enabled by default.

To enable or disable the CommandManager, select the menu "**View, Toolbars, CommandManager.**" You must have a document open to be able to turn the CommandManager on or off. For clarity, the option "Use Large Buttons with Text" has been enabled; it can be activated by right-mouse-clicking anywhere in the CommandManager and selecting the option from the pop-up menu.

Models in SolidWorks can be displayed as simple solid colors or with high quality images; depending on the video card (graphics accelerator) used, real time reflections and shadows can be displayed using "Real View" technology. For clarity purposes Real View images will be used only from time to time in this book to help the reader more easily understand the concepts presented.

One option the user may wish to change is to view dimensions flat to screen; this way, regardless of the orientation of the part, the dimensions are easier to read. This option can be found in the menu "**Tools, Options**" under the "System Options" tab, in the "Display/Selection" section. The images in this book will use the "**Display dimensions flat to screen**" option toggled on. By default, SolidWorks shows dimensions aligned to a plane, sometimes making it difficult to read dimensions and annotations.

Option turned OFF   Option turned ON

The images in your screen *may* be slightly different from this book. The images in the book were made using Windows 7 Professional and SolidWorks' default installation settings. Unless otherwise noted, the only changes made to SolidWorks' default options were adding a white background and in some instances the preview colors were changed to improve clarity in print and/or electronic format.

IMPORTANT NOTE: High resolution images of all the exercises in this book can be downloaded from our website for reference.

www.mechanicad.com

With that said, let's design something…

Part Modeling

The design process in SolidWorks generally starts in the part modeling environment, where we create the different parts that make the design of the product or machine. These are later assembled to other parts; at that time the group of parts becomes an Assembly. In SolidWorks, every component of the design will be modeled separately, and each one is a single file with the extension **.sldprt*. SolidWorks is a *Feature based software*; this means that the parts are created by incrementally adding features to the model. In the simplest of terms, features are operations that either add or remove material to a part; for example, extrusions, cuts, rounds, etc. There are also features that do not create geometry, but are used as a construction aid, such as auxiliary planes, axes, etc.

This book will cover many different features to create parts, including the most commonly used tools and options. Some features require a **Sketch** or profile to be created first; these are known as Sketched features. A Sketch is a 2D profile created on a plane or flat face using the sketch environment, that will be later used to generate a 3D feature. It is in the Sketch where most of the design information is added to the model, including dimensions and geometric relations between the different sketch elements and existing geometry. Examples of sketched features include Extrusions, Revolved features, Sweeps and Lofts.

A 2D Sketch can be created only in a Plane or planar (flat) face. By default, every SolidWorks Part and Assembly has three **default planes** (Front, Top and Right) and an Origin. Most parts can be started in any one of these planes. It is not really critical which plane we use to start our designs; however, the plane's initial selection can potentially save us a little time when working in an assembly or when we start detailing the part in the detail drawing for manufacturing.

The initial planning that takes place before we start modeling a part is called the *Design Intent.* The Design Intent basically includes the general plan of how the part is going to be modeled, sort of a *"Step 1, Step 2, etc."*, and how we anticipate (or guess) it may change to accommodate possible future design changes to fit other parts in an assembly or overall design needs. For example, we may choose to create a revolved feature instead of multiple extrusions, or the other way around, based on the particular needs of the task at hand.

SolidWorks is a 3D parametric design software. By *parametric* design, we mean that the models created are driven by parameters. These parameters are dimensions, geometric relations, equations, etc. When a parameter is modified, the 3D model is updated to reflect the changes. Good design practices are evident in how well the Design Intent and model integrity is maintained when parameters are modified. In other words, *the model updates predictably when we change the parameters*.

Notes:

The Housing

Notes:

When we start a new design, we have to decide how we are going to model it. Remember that the parts will be made one feature or operation at a time. It takes a little practice to define the optimum feature sequence for any given part, but this is something that you will master once you learn to think of parts as a sequence of features or operations. To help you understand how to make the *'Housing'* part, we'll show a sequence of features. The order of some of these features can be changed, but always remember that sometimes we have to make some features before others. For example, we cannot round a corner if there are no corners to round! A sequence will be shown at the beginning of each part, and the dimensional details will be given as we progress.

In this lesson we will cover the following tools and features: creating various sketch elements, geometric relations and dimensions, Extrusions, Cuts, Fillets, Mirror Features, Hole Wizard, Linear and Circular Patterns. For the *'Housing'*, we'll follow the next sequence of features:

Base Extrusion	Top Extrusion	Fillets	Inside Cut
Front boss	Mirror Front boss	Side boss	Mirror Side boss
Front cut	Side cut	Screw hole	Screw hole pattern
Top tapped holes	Base slot	Base slots pattern	Mirror slots pattern

1. - The first thing we need to do, after opening SolidWorks, is to make a **New Part** file. Go to the "New" document icon in the main toolbar and select it.

2. - We are now presented with the New Document dialog. (If your screen is different than this, click the "Novice" button in the lower left corner.) Now select the "Part" template, and click OK, this is where we tell SolidWorks that we want to create a Part file. Additional Part templates can be created, with different options and settings, including different units, dimensioning standards, materials, colors, etc. See the Appendix for information on how to make additional **templates** and change the document **units** to inches and/or millimeters. Using the "Advanced" option allows the user to choose from different custom templates when creating new documents instead of using the default templates.

3. - Now that we have made a new Part file, we have to start modeling the part, and the first thing we need to do is to make the extrusion for the base of the *'Housing'*. The first feature is usually one that other features can be added to or one that can be used as a starting point for our model. Select the "**Extruded Boss/Base**" icon from the CommandManager's Features tab (active by default). SolidWorks will automatically start a new **Sketch**, and we will be asked to select the plane in which we want to start working. Since this is the first feature of the part, we will be shown the three standard planes (Front, Top and Right). Remember the sketch is the 2D environment where we draw the profile before creating an extrusion, in other words, before we make it "3D."

4. - For the *'Housing'* we'll select the *"Top Plane"* to create the first sketch. We want to select the *"Top Plane"* because we are going to start modeling the part at the base of the *'Housing'* and build it up as was shown in the sequence at the beginning of this chapter. Don't get too concerned if you can't figure out which plane to choose first when starting to model a part. At worst, what you thought would be a Front view may not be the front; this is for the most part irrelevant, as the user is able to choose the views at the time of detailing the part in the 2D drawing for manufacturing. Select the *"Top Plane"* from the screen using the left mouse button. Notice the plane is highlighted as we move the mouse to it. The view orientation will be automatically rotated to a Top View.

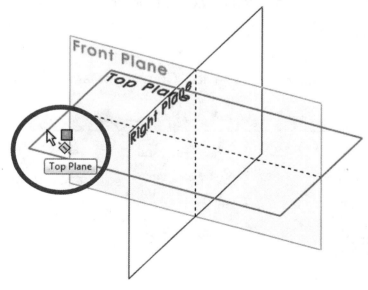

After selecting the *"Top Plane"*, a new **Sketch** is created are now we are working in the sketch environment. This is where we will create the profiles that will be used to make features like Extrusions, Cuts, etc. SolidWorks gives us many indications, most of them graphical, to help us know when we are working in the Sketch environment, like:

a) The **Confirmation Corner** is activated in the upper right corner and displays the Sketch icon in transparent colors.

b) The Status bar at the bottom shows "Editing Sketch" in the lower right corner.

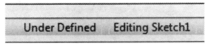

c) In the FeatureManager "Sketch1" is added at the bottom just under "Origin."

d) The part's Origin is projected in red and the grid is visible.

e) The Sketch tab is activated in the CommandManager displaying sketch tools.

f) If the "Display Grid" option is activated, it will be displayed. This can be easily turned on or off *while in the Sketch environment*, by right-mouse-clicking in the graphics area and selecting the "Display Grid."

As the reader can see, SolidWorks gives us plenty of clues to help us know when we are working in a sketch.

5. - Notice that when we make the first sketch, SolidWorks rotates the view to match the plane that we selected. In this case, we are looking at the part from *above*. By default, this is done only in the first sketch to help the user get oriented. For subsequent operations we can rotate the view manually using view orientation tools, or turn on the option to always rotate the view to be normal to the sketch plane in the menu "**Tools, Options, System Options, Sketch**" and turn on the option "**Auto-rotate view normal to sketch plane on sketch creation**." Turning this option on will help new users get oriented in 3D. Feel free to turn it ON or OFF as you feel comfortable.

6. - The first thing we need to do in the first sketch is to draw a rectangle and center it about the origin. Select the "**Rectangle**" tool from the "Sketch" tab *or* make a right-mouse-button-click in the graphics area to select it from the pop-up menu, *or* click-and-drag with the right-mouse-button to select it in the Mouse Gestures. Make sure we have the "Corner Rectangle" option selected in the Rectangle's PropertyManager.

Click-and-drag in the graphics area to draw a Rectangle around the origin as shown. Left-mouse-click-and-drag to the opposite corner. Don't worry too much about the size; we'll dimension it in a later step.

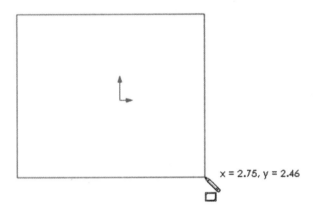

x = 2.75, y = 2.46

7. - Notice the lines are colored using the selected color defined in the system options (Tools, Options, System Options, Color) after finishing the rectangle. This means the lines are pre-selected immediately after creating them. You can unselect them by hitting the Escape (Esc) key, this will also de-select (turn off) the rectangle tool. Since we only need one rectangle in this sketch, hit the "Esc" key to finish the command. After drawing the rectangle we need to draw a "**Centerline**" from one corner of the rectangle to the opposite corner. The purpose of this line is to help us center the rectangle about the part's origin. (We'll also learn a faster way to do this in the next few steps.) From the "Sketch" tab select the Line command's drop down arrow, and select "**Centerline**" (or the menu "**Tools, Sketch Entities, Centerline**").

8. - SolidWorks gives the user indications that we will start or finish a line (or any geometric entity) at an existing endpoint using yellow icons; when we locate the cursor near an endpoint, line, edge, origin, etc. it will "snap" to it. Click in one corner of the rectangle, click in the opposite corner as shown and press the "Esc" key to complete the Centerline command.

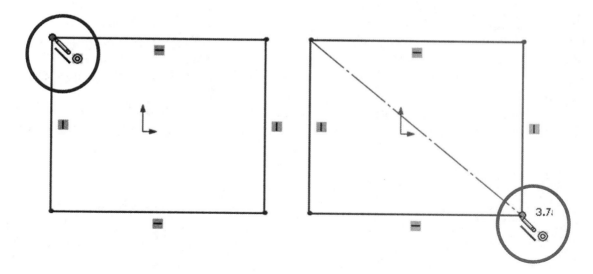

9. - Next we want to make the *midpoint* of the centerline *coincident* to the part's origin; for this step we will add a "**Midpoint**" geometric relation between the centerline we just drew and the part's origin. Select "Add Relation" from the menu "**Tools, Relations, Add**" or the "**Add Relation**" icon from the "**Display/Delete Relations**" drop-down icon. By adding this relation, the centerline's midpoint will be forced to coincide with the origin; this way the rectangle (and the part) will be centered about the origin. Centering the part about the origin and the model's planes will be useful in future operations.

 "Add Relation" can also be accessed through the right mouse button menu, or be configured to be available in the **Mouse Gestures** shortcuts.

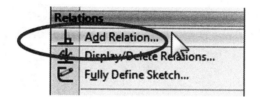

A word about the sketch right mouse button menu: The SolidWorks shortcut menu includes most of the sketch entities and commands available, making the menu very long. To improve workflow, we can customize it to only include the commands we use most frequently. To customize it, select the double down arrow at the bottom of the menu, and select "Customize Menu." The menu will change to show a checkbox next to each menu item; here we can click to turn commands on or off to fit our needs. Feel free to turn them on/off as we progress through the book to better fit your needs.

10. - The "Add Relations" PropertyManager is displayed. The **Property-Manager** is the area where we will make our selections and choice of options for most commands. Select the previously made centerline and the part's origin by clicking on them in the graphics area (notice how they change color and get listed under the "Selected Entities" box.) Click on **"Midpoint"** under the "Add Relations" box to add the relation. Now the *center* of the line is *coincident* with the Origin. Click on OK (the green checkmark) to finish the command.

To test the relation we just added, click-and-drag one corner of the rectangle. You will see the rectangle resizing symmetrically <u>and</u> centered around the origin because of the geometric relation we added.

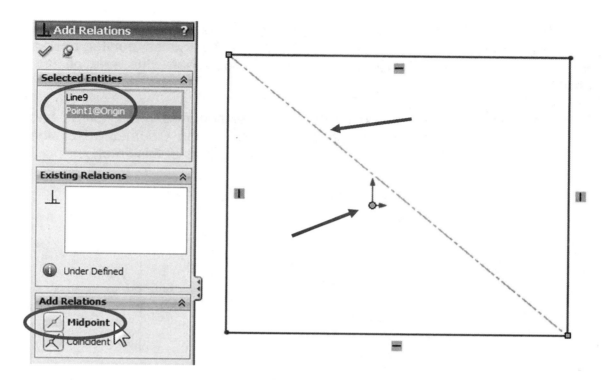

11. - What we just did is we *manually* added a **geometric relation**; we also added geometric relations *automatically* when we drew the rectangle and the centerline in the previous step. SolidWorks allows us to view the existing relations between sketch elements graphically by going to the menu "**View, Sketch Relations**", or from the "**Hide/Show Items**" drop down icon in the graphics area. This option is enabled by default.

The **Sketch Origin** defines the local Horizontal (short red arrow) and local Vertical (long red arrow) directions for the sketch. This is important to know because, when we work in 3D, we may be looking at the part in a different orientation, and vertical may not necessarily be "up" on the screen. This is a convenient way for us to know where "up" is in the sketch regardless of which way we are looking. In SolidWorks we have the following basic types of geometric relations between sketch entities:

	Vertical Parallel to the sketch vertical direction (long red arrow in the origin)
	Horizontal Parallel to the sketch horizontal direction (short red arrow in the sketch origin)
	Coincident is when an endpoint touches another line, endpoint, arc, circle or model edge.
	Midpoint is when a line's endpoint coincides with the middle of another line or a model edge. A Midpoint relation implies it is also Coincident.
	Parallel is when two or more lines or a line and a model edge are parallel to each other.
	Perpendicular is when two lines (or a line and a model edge) are 90° from each other. Vertical and horizontal lines are perpendicular. Note that the lines don't have to touch each other in order to be perpendicular.
	Concentric is when two arcs or circles share the same center. Concentric can also be between a point or line's endpoint and an arc or circle's center.
	Tangent is when a line and an arc or circle, or two arcs or circles are tangent to each other.

	Equal is when two or more lines are the same length, or two or more arcs or circles have the same diameter.
	Collinear is when two or more lines lie on the same line. They don't have to be connected.

13. - Once we have added the "Midpoint" geometric relation, the next step is to dimension the rectangle. To avoid visual clutter in the screen we can turn off the geometric relations display using the menu "**View, Sketch Relations**." Click with the right mouse button in the graphics area and select "**Smart Dimension**" from the pop-up menu or select the "Smart Dimension" icon from the Sketch toolbar. Notice the cursor changes adding a small dimension icon next to it. This icon will let us know the Smart Dimension tool is selected.

Smart Dimension can also be activated from the Mouse Gestures (default right-mouse-click-and-drag up), or assign a shortcut key using the menu "**Tools, Customize, Keyboard**." Feel free to customize a shortcut that works for you. In the next image we'll add the shortcut key "D" to Smart Dimension.

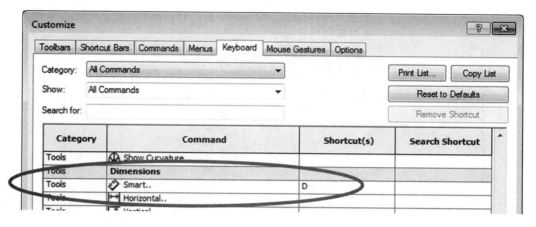

14. - Adding dimensions in SolidWorks is simple and straight forward. With the Smart Dimension tool active, click to select the right vertical line and then click just to the right to locate the dimension. SolidWorks will show the "Modify" dialog box, where we can enter the 2.625″ dimension. Repeat with the top horizontal line and enter a 6″ dimension. As soon as the dimension value is entered, the geometry updates to reflect the correct size.

 If your document is in metric units, you can override the default units by adding "in" or ″ at the end of the value in the Modify dialog box. If this is the case, type 2.625in *or* 2.625″ and 6in *or* 6″ to override the units to inches.

To change a dimension after adding it, double click on it to display the "Modify" box again. Another way to pick the units of measure is to hover the mouse in the pop-up "Units" directly under the value box and then pick the units of your choice.

 To change the document's units we can either 1) go to the menu "**Tools, Options, Document Properties, Units**", or 2) click in the status bar in the lower right corner to set the units from the quick pick menu, or 3) launch the "**Edit Document Units**..." options page to change units, decimal places, dual dimension units, etc.

Our book exercises will be using mostly inches with three decimal places unless otherwise noted.

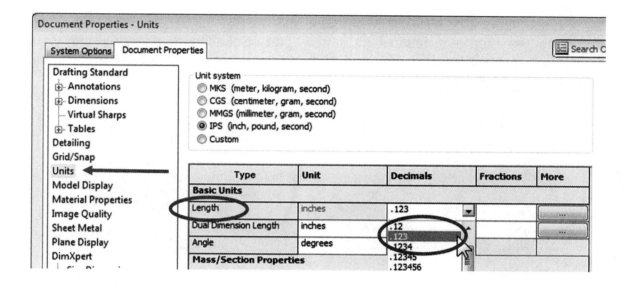

After dimensioning the lines, notice the sketch lines changed from Blue to Black. This is the way SolidWorks lets us know that the geometry is *defined*, meaning that we have added enough information (dimensions and/or geometric relations) to completely define the geometry in the sketch. The status bar also shows "Fully Defined" in the lower right corner. This is the preferred state before creating a feature, since there is no information missing and the geometry has been accurately described.

A few more words about a sketch's state. A sketch can be in one of several states; the three main ones are:

- **Under Defined**: (BLUE) Not enough dimensions and/or geometric relations have been provided to completely define the sketch. Sketch geometry is blue and lines/endpoints can be dragged with the left mouse button.

- **Fully Defined**: (BLACK) The Sketch has all the necessary dimensions and/or geometric relations to completely define it. *This is the desired state*. Fully defined geometry is black.

- **Over Defined**: (RED) Redundant and/or conflicting dimensions and/or geometric relations have been added to the sketch. If an over-defining dimension or relation is added, SolidWorks will immediately warn the user. If an over-defining geometric relation (or dimension) is added, delete it or use the menu, "**Edit, Undo**" or select the "Undo" icon. If an over-defining dimension is added, the user will be offered an option to cancel it.

15. - Now that the sketch is fully defined, we will create the first feature of the *'Housing'*; this is when we go from the 2D Sketch to a 3D feature. Select the Features tab in the CommandManager and click in the "**Extrude**" icon, or click in the "**Exit Sketch**" icon in the Sketch toolbar. In the second case, SolidWorks remembers that we wanted to make an Extrusion in the first place, and displays the Extrude command's PropertyManager after exiting the sketch. Notice that the first time we create a feature in a new part, SolidWorks changes the view orientation to an Isometric view and gives us a preview of what the feature will look like when finished.

We will make the first extrusion 0.25" thick. To do this, select the options indicated in the "**Extrude**" command. To finish the extrusion, select the OK button or press the "Enter" key.

16. - After the first extrusion is completed, notice that "Boss-Extrude1" has been added to the FeatureManager. The confirmation corner is no longer active. The status bar now reads "Editing Part" to alert us that we are now editing the part and not a sketch.

Expanding the "Boss-Extrude1" feature in the FeatureManager by clicking on the "+" on the left side of it, we see that "Sketch1" has been absorbed by the "Boss-Extrude1" feature.

 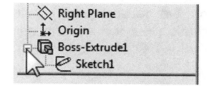

17. - The second feature will be similar to the first one, but with different dimensions. To create the second extrusion, we need to make a new sketch. When we select the **Extruded Boss/Base** in the Features tab or the **Sketch** icon in the Sketch tab, SolidWorks gives us a message in the PropertyManager asking us to select a Plane or a planar (flat) face to add the sketch to. We'll select the top face of the previous extrusion to add the sketch for the next feature.

 If a Plane or flat face is pre-selected before the command, the new Sketch is immediately created in that Plane or face without a message.

18. - When we made the first sketch, the view was automatically oriented to be normal to the sketch plane. To get subsequent sketches to be automatically oriented normal to the sketch plane and saving us from doing it manually, we can set the option "**Auto-rotate view normal to sketch plane on sketch creation**" found in the menu "**Tools, Options, Sketch**."

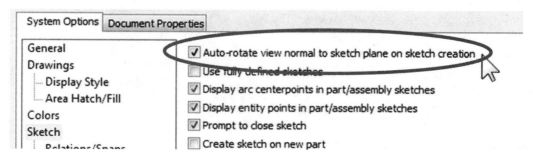

If you are not looking at the part from the Top view after selecting the top face, or chose *not* to turn on the option, manually change to a **Top View** to see the part from the top using the "**View Orientation**" icon or the default shortcut "**Ctrl+5**", as indicated in the tooltip. Notice that when we place the mouse over a view orientation, we get a pop-up preview of it. In SolidWorks we are free to work in any orientation we like as long as we can see what we are doing. Re-orienting the view helps us get used to 3D in a more familiar way by looking at it in 2D.

19. - Notice that after starting the second sketch, the Sketch tab in the CommandManager is selected. For the second sketch we'll use the "**Center Rectangle**" command. Click in the Rectangle's tool drop down menu in the Sketch tab, and select "**Center Rectangle**"; if you selected the rectangle as before, you can change the rectangle type to "**Center Rectangle**" from the Rectangle's PropertyManager, too.

To make a Center Rectangle click in the Origin first, then on the top edge of the first extrusion (or the bottom; it really doesn't matter) to finish it. Notice the yellow Coincident icon as the pointer is in the origin and then on the model edge. By doing the rectangle this way we automatically add coincident relations to the origin and the top edge. The "**Center Rectangle**" command saves us from adding the centerlines and midpoint relations making the rectangle centered about the origin in a single operation.

20. - Select the "**Smart Dimension**" tool (toolbar, right mouse menu, Mouse Gesture or keyboard shortcut), and dimension the rectangle 4″ wide by selecting the top (or bottom) line and locating the dimension as shown. Adding this dimension will fully define the sketch since we had automatically added geometric relations when the rectangle was created.

 Note: The assigned keyboard shortcut ("D") is displayed in the tooltip.

21. - We are now ready to make the second extruded feature. Select the "**Extrude**" command in the Features tab of the CommandManager (or "**Exit Sketch**" if you initially selected "**Extrude**") and make the extrusion 3.5″ high. Also notice the part does not rotate to show an isometric view as it did in the first extrusion, and there is no option to make it do so. Therefore, we have to rotate the view ourselves to see a preview. From the Standard Views icon, select the **Isometric** view ("Ctrl+7" shortcut or Mouse Gesture) to see the preview of the second extrusion. Click OK to complete the command.

22. - The next step is to round the edges of the two extrusions. To do this, we will select the **Fillet** command. The Fillet is what's called an applied feature; we don't need a sketch to create it, and it's applied directly to the solid model. Select the "**Fillet**" icon from the Features Tab of the CommandManager. By default, "**Constant Radius**" type is selected. Change the radius to 0.25″ and select the eight vertical corners indicated in the preview. SolidWorks highlights the model edges when we place the cursor on top of them to let us know what we'll be selecting. If an edge to be selected is not visible, rotate the model using the menu "**View, Modify, Rotate**." ⟳ Rotate Click-and-drag in the graphics area to rotate. Another way to rotate the model is by holding down the middle mouse button (scroll wheel), and dragging in the graphics area or using the arrow keys. Click OK when all eight edges are selected to complete the command.

 To use the mouse wheel's button to rotate the model, you *may* have to configure the middle button to change it from the default "Scroll" mode to "Middle Mouse Button."

 If a model edge or face is mistakenly selected, simply click on it again to de-select it.

Select the "Full preview" option to see the resulting fillets in the graphics area as we select the edges.

A handy feature is a "**Magnifying Glass**" to selectively zoom in only one area of the model. To activate it, use the default shortcut "G" in the keyboard. To make multiple selections with it, hold down the "Ctrl" key, otherwise, the Magnifying Glass will turn off after making the first selection or after pressing "G" again. Scrolling with the mouse wheel will zoom inside the Magnifying Glass for more or less magnification.

Alternative: Instead of selecting the Fillet command first and then selecting the edges to round, we can select one or more model edges (using the Ctrl key while selecting) and *then* select the Fillet command from the fly-out features toolbar.

23. - Repeat the **Fillet** command to add a 0.125″ radius fillet at the base of the *'Housing'* but instead of edges we'll select the faces indicated. When we select a face, SolidWorks rounds all the edges connected to it. Click OK to continue.

Notice how the new fillets blend with the previous vertical fillets.

 We can change the appearance of tangent edges (The edges where two tangent faces meet) by selecting the menu, "**View, Display**" and selecting the display option desired: **Visible**, as **Phantom** or **Removed**. Explore the different options to find the one you feel more comfortable with. In this book Phantom lines will be used for clarity, unless otherwise noted.

24. - We will now remove material from the model using the "**Extruded Cut**" command. Switch to a **Top View** using the View Orientation toolbar, Mouse Gesture or shortcut Ctrl+5.

Select "**Extruded Cut**" from the Features tab; you will be asked to select a face or planar face just as with the "**Extruded Boss**." Select the top most face to create a new Sketch, and using the "**Corner Rectangle**" tool from the now visible "**Sketch**" toolbar, draw a rectangle *inside* the top face.

If the option "**Auto-rotate view normal to sketch plane on sketch creation**" is set, the model will automatically rotate to a Top View after selecting the top face.

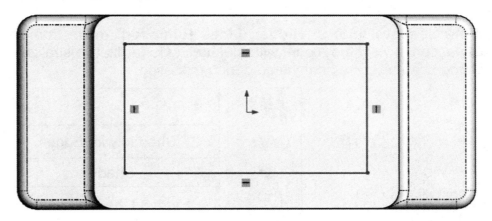

25. - To add the dimensions select the "**Smart Dimension**" tool; we can add dimensions from sketch geometry to model edges simply by selecting them. Select a Sketch line, click on a model edge parallel to it, and finally click to locate the dimension in the screen. You will be asked to enter the dimension as before. Repeat to add the rest of the dimensions.

First selection   Second Selection   Locate and enter dimension

If needed, switch to a "**Hidden Lines Removed**" mode from the **View Style** icon to view the model without shading to facilitate visualization. This change can be done at any time during modeling.

	Shaded with Edges
	Shaded
	Hidden Lines Removed
	Hidden Lines Visible
	Wireframe

26. - In this feature, we will round the corners in the sketch using a **Sketch Fillet**. We can add the fillets as applied features like before, but in this step we chose to show you how to round the corners in the Sketch *before* making the "Extruded Cut" feature. Select the "**Sketch Fillet**" icon from the Sketch toolbar.

Set the fillet radius to 0.150″, and click on the corners of the sketch lines as indicated to round them. Notice the preview in the screen. After clicking on all 4 corners, click OK to finish the Sketch Fillet command. Adding multiple fillets at the same time results in only one dimension being added; the reason is that SolidWorks adds an equal relation from each fillet to the dimensioned one.

After adding the sketch fillets, we can see the number of geometric relations are starting to clutter the screen. To help clear up the screen, we can turn off geometric relations. Select the menu "**View, Sketch Relations**," or from the "Hide/Show Items" dropdown icon, turn off "View Sketch Relations."

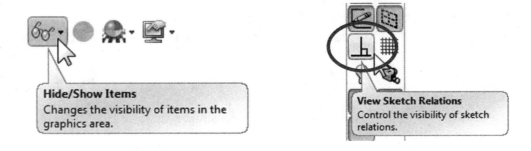

27. - Now we select the "**Extruded Cut**" icon from the Features tab in the CommandManager to remove material. Opposite to the Boss Extrude feature that adds material, the Cut feature, as its name implies, removes material from the model.

Extruded Cut
Cuts a solid model by extruding a sketched profile in one or two directions.

Change the view to Isometric ....

...and **Shaded with Edges** for better visualization.

Make the cut 3.5″ deep and click on OK to finish the cut.

 Features can be **Renamed** in the FeatureManager for easier identification. To rename a feature, slowly double-click the feature, or select it and press F2, and type a new name (just like renaming files in Windows Explorer.)

| Select Feature | Click again...(or F2) | Type a new name | Finish |

28. - In the next step we will add a round boss to the front of the *'Housing'*. Switch to a **Front View** using the "View Orientation" toolbar, Mouse Gestures or shortcut Ctrl+1.

Select the "**Sketch**" icon from the Sketch tab in the CommandManager and click in the front face, or, the reverse order: select the face first, and then click in the "**Sketch**" icon.

29. - Once we have the sketch created select the "**Circle**" tool from the Sketch tab in the CommandManager or the Mouse Gestures. Draw a circle approximately as shown; click near the middle of the part to locate the center of the circle, and click again to set its size. (You can also click-and-drag from the center to draw the circle.) Don't worry about the size; we'll dimension it next.

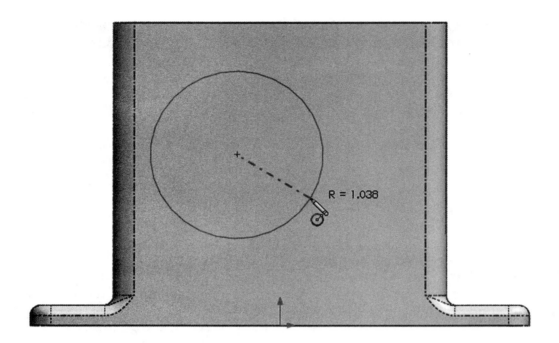

R = 1.038

To define the circle's location, select the "**Smart Dimension**" tool, click on either the center of the circle or its perimeter, and then on the top edge of the *'Housing'*. Finally locate the dimension and enter the value of 1.875″. For the Diameter, select the circle and locate the 3.25″ diameter dimension as shown.

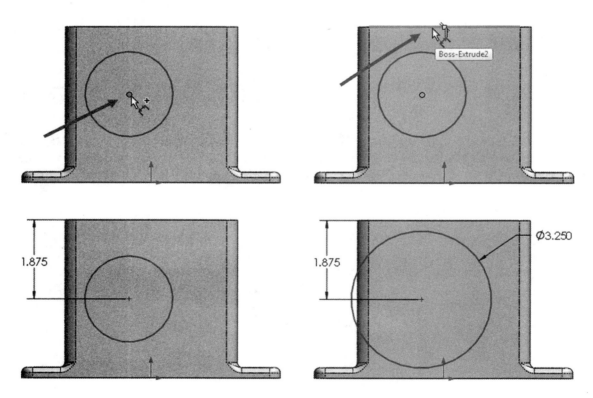

30. - To make the circle horizontally centered in the part, we will manually add a **Vertical Relation** between the center of the circle and the part's origin. SolidWorks allows us to align sketch elements to each other or to existing model geometry (edges, faces, vertices, planes, origin, etc.) From the right mouse button menu, select "**Add Relation**" or use the menu "**Tools, Relations, Add.**"

Select <u>the circle's center</u> (not the perimeter!) and the origin. Click on "**Vertical**" to add the relation and **OK** to finish. Adding this relation fully defines our sketch.

 Alternatively we can add the vertical relation by pre-selecting the origin and the circle's center, and then selecting the "Vertical" relation from the pop-up menu.

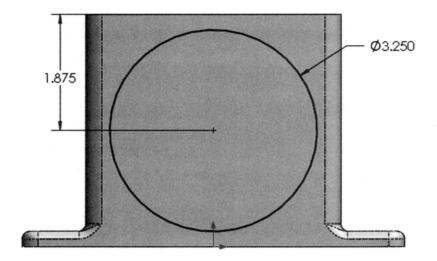

31. - Instead of making an extrusion like we did before, we are going to add material using a different technique. After adding the **Vertical** geometric relation exit the sketch. We'll use a time saving feature called "**Instant 3D**" to make the extrusion. It should be active by default in the Features tab in the CommandManager; otherwise, simply click to activate it.

To make the extrusion, switch to an isometric view using the View Orientation toolbar; select the circle of the previously made sketch. Be aware that now we are editing the part, we left the sketch editing environment. Once the sketch circle is selected, click-and-drag on the arrow that appears in it; this is the handle to extrude the sketch. You will immediately see a dynamic ruler that will show the size of the extrusion as you drag it. Make sure to extrude it 0.250". When you release the handle, a new extrusion will be created. To modify this extrusion, simply select the front face of the extrusion and drag again on the handle to its new size.

 You can control the size with more precision by dragging the handle over the ruler's marks, this way the handle will snap to them.

The smaller step in the ruler is controlled by the default increment in the spin box settings. Go to the menu "Tools, Options, Spin Box Increments." For convenience, we have set the length increment to 0.125" and 2.5mm

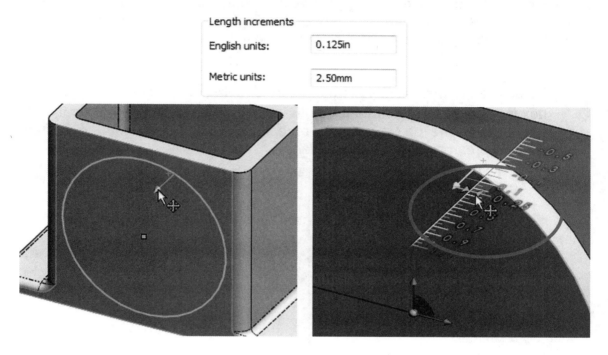

Length increments	
English units:	0.125in
Metric units:	2.50mm

32. - Rename this extrusion as "*Front Boss*" by slowly double-clicking the feature's name in the FeatureManager, or selecting it and then pressing F2.

33. - The next step is to create an identical extrusion on the opposite side of the '*Housing*'. To make it we'll use the "**Mirror**" command. It will make an identical 3D copy of the extrusion we just made. Switch to an Isometric view to help us visualize the Mirror's preview and make sure we are getting what we want. Select the "**Mirror**" icon from the Features toolbar in the CommandManager.

34. - From the Mirror's PropertyManager, we have to make two selections. The first one is the Mirror Face or Plane and the second is the feature(s) we want to make a mirror of. The face or plane that will be used to mirror the feature has to be in the middle between the original feature and the desired mirrored copy. Making the first extrusion centered about the origin caused the "*Front Plane*" to be in the middle of the part, making it the best (and only) option for a Mirror Plane.

 To select the "*Front Plane*" (make sure the "**Mirror Face/Plane**" selection box is highlighted, this means it is the active selection box), click on the "**+**" sign next to the part's name to reveal a **fly-out FeatureManager**, from where we can select the "*Front Plane.*"

35. - After selecting the "*Front Plane*" from the fly-out FeatureManager, SolidWorks automatically activates the "**Features to Mirror**" selection box (now highlighted) and is ready for us to select the feature(s) we want to mirror. If the '*Front Boss*' extrusion is pre-selected before we activate the Mirror command, it will be added automatically to the "Features to Mirror" selection box, otherwise we will have to select it either from the FeatureManager or in the graphics area.

 When selecting features from the graphics area be sure to select a face that belongs to the feature. When traversing the FeatureManager, notice how SolidWorks highlights the features in the screen before selecting it.

Notice the preview after making your selections and click OK. Rotate the view to inspect the mirrored feature.

36. - In the next step we'll add the small boss at the right side of the *'Housing'*. Switch to a **Right view** using the View Orientation toolbar (Shortcut Ctrl+4), and select the "**Sketch**" icon from the CommandManager's Sketch tab.

Select the rightmost face to create the Sketch (or select the face and then the Sketch command), draw a circle using the "**Circle**" tool and add the dimensions shown. Just as we did with the front cylindrical boss, add a **Vertical Relation** between the center of the circle and the part's origin.

From the right mouse button menu or the Sketch toolbar, select "**Add Relation**", select the center of the circle and the origin, and add a "Vertical" relation between them by selecting it in the "Add Relations" box.

Select Sketch plane   Draw & dimension circle   Add vertical relation

 When adding relations, if you accidentally select more entities than needed, you can unselect them in the screen, or select them in the selection box and delete them using the "Delete" key.

37. - Now we are ready to extrude the sketch to make the side boss. We'll use the "**Instant 3D**" function as we did in the previous extrusion. Exit the Sketch by selecting "**Exit Sketch**" in the CommandManager's Sketch tab or the Sketch icon in the confirmation corner (*not* the red X), and change to an Isometric view. In the graphics area select the circle of the sketch we just drew, and click-and-drag the arrow along the ruler markers to make the extrusion 0.5″ long. Rename this extrusion *'Side Boss'* in the FeatureManager.

38. - Just like we did with the front circular boss, we'll mirror this extrusion about the *"Right Plane"* (which is also in the middle of the part.) Select the "**Mirror**" command from the Features tab in the CommandManager and, using the fly-out FeatureManager, select the *"Right Plane"* as the "**Mirror Face/Plane**" and the *'Side Boss'* extrusion in the "**Features to Mirror**" selection box to complete the Mirror command.

39. - We'll now make the circular cut in the front of the *'Housing'*. Change to a Front view for easier visualization. Select the "**Sketch**" icon from the Sketch tab and click in the round front face of the part (Or select the face first, and then the Sketch icon.)

Draw a circle using the "**Circle**" tool and dimension it 2.250″ diameter.

To locate the circle in the center of the circular face, we'll add a "**Concentric Relation**." Select the "**Add Relation**" icon from the right mouse button menu; select the circle we just drew and the edge of the circular face. Click "**Concentric**" to add the relation and center the circle. Click **OK** to finish the command.

 Another way to add a concentric relation is to pre-select the circle and the edge of the "*Front Boss*" (hold down the **Ctrl** key while selecting), and select **Concentric** either from the pop-up menu or the PropertyManager. When adding a single geometric relation this is a faster way to do it.

40. - Now that the circle is concentric with the boss, we'll make the cut. Select the "**Extruded Cut**" command from the Features tab and switch to an isometric view for better visualization. From the "**Extruded Cut**" properties select the "**Through All**" option and OK to finish; by using this end condition the cut will go through the entire part regardless of its size. In other words, *if* we change the *'Housing'* to be wider, the cut will still go through it.

41. - We will now make a hole in the boss added in step 37 for a shaft. Switch to a Right view and create a new sketch on the small circular face of the "*Side Boss*" by selecting the "**Sketch**" icon and then the circular face to locate it.

We know that we want the hole to be concentric with the boss. In order to do this we can draw the circle and add a concentric relation as we did before; however, this is a two step process. Instead, we will do it in one step as follows: Select the "**Circle**" tool icon and *before* drawing the circle, move the cursor and rest it on top of the circular edge as shown, the center of the circular edge is revealed in a fraction of a second. DO NOT CLICK ON THE EDGE. This highlight works only if you have a drawing tool active (Line, Circle, Arc, etc.) This technique can be used to reveal any circular edge's center and reference any other model edges.

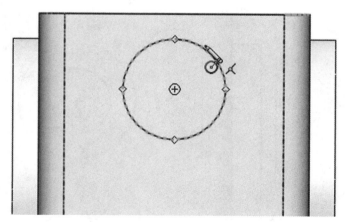

42. - Once the circular edge's center is revealed, click in it to start drawing the circle automatically capturing a concentric relation with the center of the boss. Finish the circle and dimension it 0.575″ diameter. Now the sketch is fully defined.

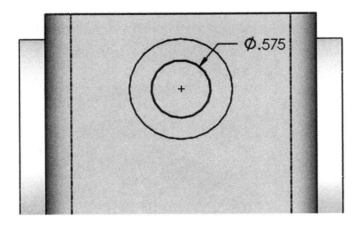

43. - Since this hole will be used for a shaft, we need to add a bilateral **tolerance** to the dimension. Select the 0.575″ dimension in the graphics area, and from the dimension's PropertyManager, under "Tolerance/Precision" select "Bilateral." Now we can add the tolerances. Notice that the dimension changes immediately in the graphics area. This tolerance will be transferred to the *Housing's* detail drawing later on. If needed, tolerances can also be added later in the detail drawing.

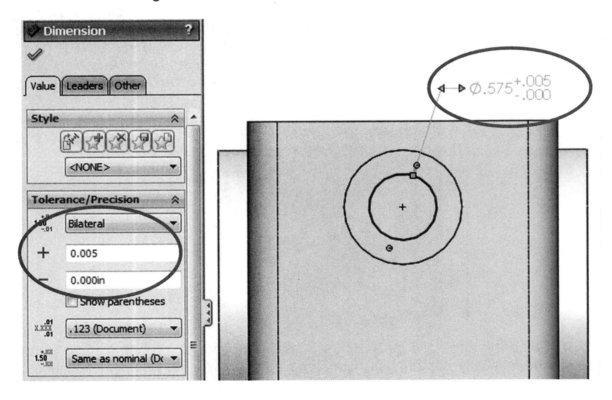

44. - Now we can make a Cut with the "**Through All**" option using the "**Extruded Cut**" command. When finished rename the Feature *"Shaft hole."*

45. - Another way to do this cut is using the "Instant 3D" feature. To use "Instant 3D" to make a cut, click in the "**Exit Sketch**" icon, change to an Isometric view for clarity, and just like we did for the Extrusion, select the sketch circle and click-and-drag the handle _into_ the part. You'll see how the part is cut as the arrow is dragged. The only disadvantage to making the cut using this technique is that the "Through All" option is not available.

46. - For the next feature we'll make a ¼"-20 tapped hole in the front face. SolidWorks provides us with a tool to automate the creation of simple, Countersunk and Counterbore holes, tap and Pipe taps by selecting a fastener size, depth and location. The "**Hole Wizard**" command is a two-step process: in the first step we define the hole's type and size, and in the second step we define the location of the hole(s). To add the tapped hole, switch to a Front view. The **Hole Wizard** is a special type of feature that uses 2 sketches that are automatically created, so there is no need to add a sketch first; in fact, it works very much like an applied feature.

Change to a Front View for clarity, and select the "**Hole Wizard**" icon from the Features tab in the CommandManager. The first thing we'll do is to define the hole's type and size. Select "**Tap**" for "Hole Type", "ANSI Inch" for Standard, "Tapped Hole" for Screw type and from the drop down selection list pick "¼-20" for size. Change the "End Condition" to "Up to Next", this will make the tapped hole's depth up to the next face where it makes a complete round hole. At the bottom activate the button to add **Cosmetic Threads**.

47. - The second step of the "**Hole Wizard**" is to define the hole's location. After selecting the type of hole we want to make, activate the "**Positions**" tab at the top of the properties, SolidWorks will ask to select a flat face to locate the hole(s). Select the round face at the front of the part.

Immediately after selecting the face, SolidWorks will automatically select the "**Sketch Point**" tool and we are ready to define the hole's location. Anywhere we add a sketch point, the Hole Wizard will add a hole. For this exercise we only need to make one, and in order to locate it we'll use regular sketch tools (dimensions and geometric relations; notice that we are working in a Sketch.) We want this hole to be located in the middle of the flat face's width; to locate, first

draw a "**Centerline**" by selecting it from the drop-down menu in the "**Line**" command. Start drawing the centerline at the right quadrant of the outer circular edge, and finish it in the same quadrant of the inner circular edge. The quadrants will be activated after selecting the Centerline tool and touching (not clicking!) the circular edge. (Notice the reference icons after touching the edges.) Hit the Esc key once to finish the Centerline command.

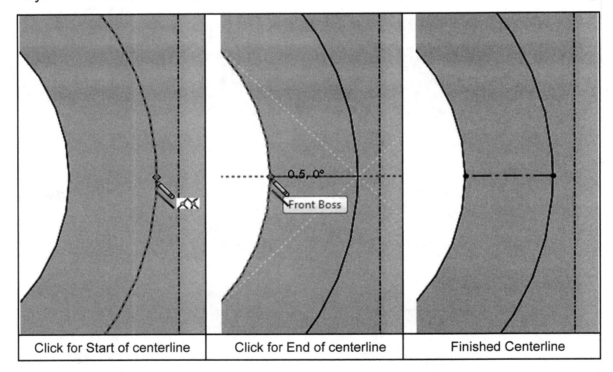

| Click for Start of centerline | Click for End of centerline | Finished Centerline |

When the centerline is complete, select the "**Sketch Point**" from the Sketch tab in the CommandManager. The idea behind this technique is to make sure the hole is centered in the circular face. To add a sketch point and define the hole's location, touch the centerline for a split second to reveal its midpoint (like we just did with the circular edges), and click in its center to add the sketch point.

Now the hole will be located in the middle of the Centerline. Click OK to finish the Hole Wizard.

 If the point had been added in a different location, we could add the midpoint relation by Window-Selecting the "**Point**" and the "**Centerline**", and from the pop-up toolbar selecting "**Make Midpoint**." If we had pre-selected the face before selecting the hole wizard command we would have seen this scenario.

Window select entities   Add Midpoint relation from pop-up menu

 The "Cosmetic Thread" option adds a threaded texture to the holes, instead of an actual thread for looks and performance purposes. To change the "Cosmetic Threads" display right-mouse-click in the "*Annotations*" folder at the top of the FeatureManager, select Details and activate the options "Cosmetic Threads" and "Shaded Cosmetic Threads." Remember that there are no real threads in the model. It can be done, but it's mostly unnecessary in these cases. We'll learn how to model a real thread later.

The difference between the two types is:

- *Cosmetic thread* is the annotation that shows up in a 2D drawing to indicate a thread.
- *Shaded cosmetic thread* is a texture added to the holes to give the 3D model the appearance of a thread and its only for visual effect.

This is the finished ¼"-20 Tapped Hole with cosmetic threads.

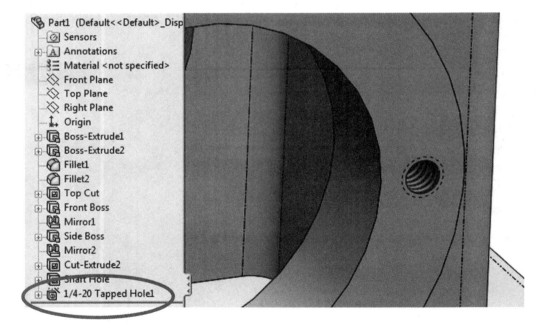

48. - After making the Tapped hole, we suddenly realize that the walls of the *'Housing'* need to be thinner, and need to make a change to our design. In order to do this, we find the feature that we want to modify in the FeatureManager (*'Top Cut'* in our case) or in the graphics area, and select it. From the pop-up toolbar, select the **"Edit Sketch"** icon. This will allow us to go back to the original sketch and make changes to it. Notice the selected feature is highlighted in the screen.

There is no real purpose to this dimensional change but to show the reader how to change an existing feature's sketch if needed. While editing a sketch, dimensions, geometry and geometric relations can be added, edited or removed as needed.

 Selecting the "Edit Feature" icon will show the Cut Extrude command options; this is where we can change the cut's depth and other feature's parameters.

 If we select the feature with a right-mouse-click, we will see the pop-up toolbar along with an options menu. The most commonly used commands are already in the pop-up toolbar

If the "**Instant 3D**" command is activated, selecting a feature will show its dimensions on the screen (more about that later.)

49. - What we just did was to go back to editing the feature's Sketch, just like when we first created it. Switch to a Top view if needed for visualization. To change a dimension's value double click on it to display the "Modify" dialog box. Change the two dimensions indicated from 0.375″ to 0.25″ as shown.

 To arrange the dimensions just click-and-drag to move them around.

50. - After changing the dimensions we cannot select "**Cut Extrude**" because we had already made a cut; what we have to do now is to "**Exit Sketch**" or "**Rebuild**" the part (Ctrl+B) to update the model with the new dimensions.

 Another way we can make these changes is using the "**Instant3D**" functionality. The way it works is very simple: instead of having to edit the sketch, we select the feature that we want to modify either in the FeatureManager or the graphics area (in this case one of the inside faces which were made with the Cut Extrude) and click-and-drag the **blue dots** at each of the dimensions that need to be modified until we get the desired value, without having to edit the sketch. Dragging the mouse pointer over the ruler markers will give you values in exact increments. Depending on the speed of your PC and the feature being modified, Instant3D may be slow, as the model is being dynamically updated.

A third option to change the dimensions is to click on the dimension's value and type a new one. If Instant3D is not active, double-click the dimension to change the value; after making the dimension changes we need to Rebuild the model.

51. - Now we will add more tapped holes to complete the flange's mounting holes. We'll use the first hole as a "seed" to make copies of it using the "**Circular Pattern**" command. In the Features tab, select the drop-down list below the "**Linear Pattern**" to reveal the drop down menu and select "**Circular Pattern**" or use the menu "**Insert, Pattern/Mirror, Circular Pattern**." Note that commands are grouped by similar functionality.

52. - The "**Circular Pattern**" needs a circular edge, a cylindrical surface or an axis as a reference for the direction of the circular pattern. Click inside the Parameters selection box to activate it, and then select the edge indicated for the pattern axis.

53. - Any circular edge or cylindrical face that share the same axis can be used for a direction, as shown in the following images.

Another option for Pattern Axis is a temporary axis. Each cylindrical surface has a "Temporary Axis" that runs through its center. To see them select the menu "**View, Temporary Axes**" or in the "Hide/Show Items" toolbar.

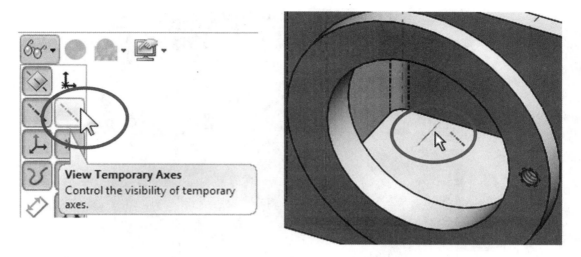

54. - After selecting the Pattern Axis click inside the "**Features to Pattern**" selection box to activate it (Notice it gets highlighted.) Select the *"¼-20 Tapped Hole1"* feature from the fly-out FeatureManager; change the number of copies to six (this value includes the original), and make sure the "Equal spacing" option is selected to equally space the copies in 360 degrees. Notice the preview in the graphics area and click OK to finish the command.

 The feature to be patterned can also be selected from the graphics area; in this case <u>a face of the feature</u> needs to be selected. Sometimes a face can be difficult to select because it may be small, like this hole. In this case, we can use the "**Magnifying Glass**" (Shortcut "G") to make selection easier.

Direction 1
| Spacing: | 360deg |
| Instances: | 6 |

1/4-20 Tapped Hole1

55. - Since we need to have the same six tapped holes in the other side of the *'Housing'*, we will use the **"Mirror"** command to copy the Circular Pattern about the *"Front Plane."* Make this mirror about the *"Front Plane"* and mirror the *"CircPattern1"* feature created in the previous step. Click OK to finish.

After the mirror, your part should look like this:

56. - We will now add four #6-32 tapped holes to the topmost face using the **Hole Wizard**. Switch to a Top view (Ctrl+5 or Mouse Gestures) for visibility and select the "**Hole Wizard**" icon.

57. - In the Hole Wizard's PropertyManager, select the "**Tap**" Hole Specification icon, and select the options shown for a #6-32 Tapped Hole. The "Blind" condition tells SolidWorks to make the hole an exact depth.

58. - Click in the "Positions" tab to define the hole locations. Select the top face to add the holes, and notice that immediately after we select the face the "**Sketch Point**" tool is automatically selected, we are editing a sketch and the Sketch toolbar is activated.

59. - With the "**Point**" tool active, *touch* each of the round corner edges to reveal their centers, and then click in their centers to add a point in each one; this way we'll make the points concentric to each corner fillet's center. Click OK to finish the Hole Wizard.

Touch the edge   Click on Center   Point added

60. - We are now ready to make the slots at the base of the *'Housing'*. For this task it will be easier to switch to a Top view. To add a new sketch, we can select the **"Sketch"** command and click on the selected face as before, but in this case we'll learn how to use the pop-up toolbar. Select the face, and from the pop-up toolbar, select **"Sketch."** Notice there are two similar icons, the one on top is **"Edit Sketch"** and is used to modify the sketch of the feature we selected, the one below is **"Sketch"** to create a new sketch on the selected flat face.

 If **"Edit Sketch"** is selected instead of **"Sketch"**, simply click on the red "X" in the confirmation corner in the upper right corner of the graphics area to cancel any changes made to the sketch and go back to editing the model.

To make the slot, we'll use the **"Straight Slot"** command from the Sketch tab in the CommandManager. This tool will create a slot by first drawing the centerline and then defining the width of the slot. Select the **"Straight Slot"** icon and activate the "Add Dimensions" option, it will automatically add dimensions when we finish. First click to locate the center of one arc, click to locate the second, and click a third time to define the width. When finished, double click the dimensions to change them and make the slot 0.375″ long and 0.250″ wide.

Add dimension option   Locate first center   Locate second Center

Define slot width   Automatic dimensions   Corrected dimensions

 The "**Slot**" command has more options, including arc slots and overall slot length dimension.

 To enable auto dimension while adding sketch geometry, select the menu "**Tools, Options, System Options, Sketch**" and activate:

☑ Enable on screen numeric input on entity creation

Another way to activate the option is by right-mouse-click (with a sketch tool active) and turn on "**Sketch Numeric Input**." This option will allow you to type the dimensions (entity size) as you sketch. To also add the dimensions, do a second right-mouse-click and turn on the option "**Add Dimension**."

After the slot is defined, locate the bottom of the slot by adding two 0.5″ dimensions to the lower and left edges of the base as shown. Finish the slot by making an "**Extruded Cut**" using the "Through All" option. Rename this feature "*Slot*."

61. - We will now create a "**Linear Pattern**" of the slot. A linear pattern allows us to make copies of one or more features along one or two directions (usually along model edges.) Select the "**Linear Pattern**" command from the Features tab in the CommandManager.

 Using the Mirror command keeps the design intent better, but we chose to show the user how to use the Linear Pattern function instead.

62. - In the Linear Pattern's Property-Manager, the "Direction 1" selection box is active; select the edge indicated for the direction of the copies. The copies will follow this direction. Any linear edge can be used as long as it is in the desired direction of the pattern.

Once the edge is selected, an arrow indicates the direction in which the copies will be made. If the Direction Arrow in the graphics area is pointing in the wrong direction click in the "**Reverse Direction**" button next to the "Direction 1" selection box.

63. - Now click inside the "Features to Pattern" selection box to activate it and select the slot feature either from the fly-out FeatureManager or the graphics area. Change the spacing between the copies to 1.25″ and total copies to 2. This value includes the original just like in the Circular Pattern. Click OK to finish the command.

64. - We need the slots on both sides, so we'll copy the previous linear pattern to the other side of the *'Housing'* using the "**Mirror**" command about the "*Right Plane*." Click on the "**Mirror**" icon in the Features tab of the CommandManager; select the "*Right Plane*" as the mirror plane and the "*LPattern1*" in the "Features to Mirror" selection box to copy the slots.

Selecting the Linear Pattern feature for the mirror also includes the "seed" feature ("*Slot*").

65. - Using the "**Fillet**" command from the Features tab, add a 0.125″ radius fillet to the edges indicated as a finishing touch. Rotate the model using the middle mouse button and/or change the display style to "Hidden Lines Visible" mode to make selection easier. Click OK to finish.

66. - Now that the model is finished, we can easily determine its physical properties, such as **Weight, Volume, Center of Mass and Moments of Inertia**. SolidWorks includes a built in materials library with many different metals and alloys, plastics, woods, composite materials and others like air, glass and water.

The library includes mechanical and thermal properties such as:

- Mass density
- Elastic and Shear modulus
- Tensile, Compressive and Yield strengths
- Poisson's ratio
- Thermal expansion coefficient
- Thermal conductivity
- Specific heat

 These properties are used by SolidWorks to determine a part's weight, or determine if a component will fail under a given set of loading conditions using SimulationXpress (the built in structural analysis software.)

To assign a material to a component, right-mouse-click in the "**Material**" icon at the top of the FeatureManager, and either select "Edit Material" or pick one of the materials listed. The favorites list can be changed in the "Favorites" tab in the Materials library. For this part select "Cast Alloy Steel" from the "Steel" library. Click on "Apply" to accept the material and Close the library.

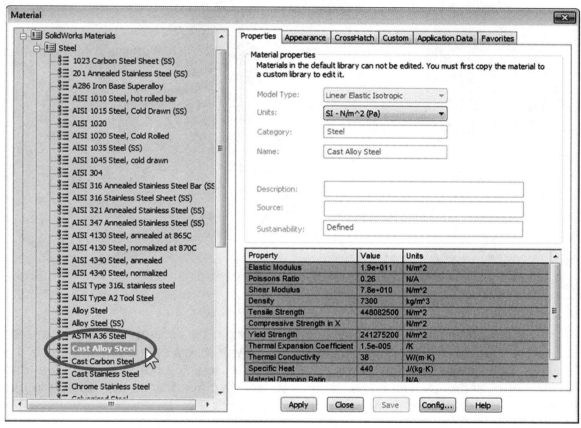

Now the FeatureManager reads "*Cast Alloy Steel*" instead of "*Material.*" Select "**Mass Properties**" from the Evaluate tab in the CommandManager. We'll see the Density (provided by the material selection), Mass (Calculated from the volume and density), Volume, Surface Area and Center of Mass coordinates relative to the origin (also indicated by a magenta triad in the graphics area), Principal Axes of inertia and Moments of inertia about the Center of Mass and the part's origin all listed in a new window, were we can copy the text for later use in reports.

Mass properties are referenced to the origin by default, but they can also be referenced to a user defined coordinate system by selecting one from the "Output coordinate system" drop down list. In the "Options" button we can change the units we want the results to be displayed with, by default mass properties are displayed using the document's units.

Save the finished part as *'Housing'* and close the file.

Exercises: Build the following parts using the knowledge acquired in this lesson. Try to use the most efficient method to complete the model. High resolution images can be found at www.mechanicad.com/download

Exercise 1
DIMENSIONS: INCHES
MATERIAL: AISI 1020

Use default settings
for 1/2"-20 ANSI Thread

2.000

2.000

R1.000

∅1.500

2.500

.375

6.500

5.000

.250

Exercise 2
DIMENSIONS: INCHES
MATERIAL: 6061 Alloy

6.000

∅.750

R.500

.250

.500 TYP.

4.500

1.250 TYP.

1.000

.500

.500

2.000

1.500

Exercise 3
DIMENSIONS: Millimeters
MATERIAL: Copper

50

15

R2.5 TYP.

45

Ø20

Ø115

M12x1.5 Tapped Hole
Default depth settings
(4X)

Ø80

Ø150

25

Exercise 4
DIMENSIONS: Millimeters
MATERIAL: ABS

130

10

10

10

10

30
TYP.

R5

20   40

160

M6x1.0 Tapped Hole
Default depth (2X)

40

R10   15   15

40

25

Engine Project Parts: Make the following components to build the engine. Save the parts using the name provided. High resolution images at mechanicad.com.

2X ⌀ .266 THRU ALL
⌴ ⌀ .563 ▼ .165

Connecting Rod Bottom
DIMENSIONS: INCHES
MATERIAL: Plain Carbon Steel

1.150

⌀1.750   ⌀1.000

R.125   .375

.750

5.500

3.785

⌀.400

R.250

Cylinder Gasket
DIMENSIONS: INCHES
MATERIAL: VITON

2.818

4.000

R.500

⌀3.150

.020

Head Gasket
DIMENSIONS: INCHES
MATERIAL: VITON

Ø3.550

Ø.340

Ø.750

R.500

Ø2.750

.025

The Side Cover

Notes:

In making the *'Side Cover'* part we will learn the following features and commands: Revolved Feature, Sketch Trim and Extend and construction geometry. We will also review some of the commands previously learned in the *'Housing'* part. The sequence of features we'll follow for the *'Side Cover'* is:

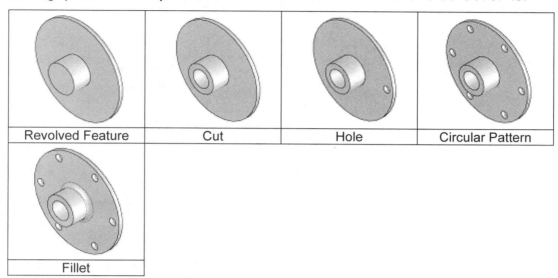

Revolved Feature	Cut	Hole	Circular Pattern

Fillet

67. - Let's make a new part. Select the "**Part**" template and click OK. Be sure to change the units to Inches and three decimal places.

The first feature we'll create is a **Revolved Feature**. As its name implies, it is created by revolving a sketch about an axis. Select the "**Revolved Boss/Base**" icon from the Features tab in the CommandManager. When asked to select a plane for the sketch, select the "*Right Plane*" (no particular reason to choose this plane except to have a good looking isometric view ☺.)

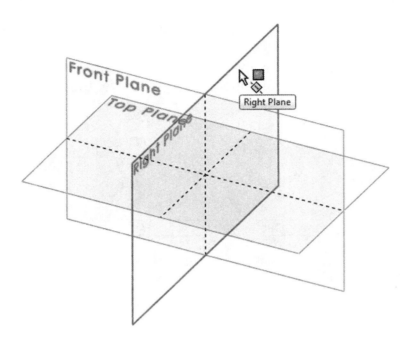

68. - Select the "**Rectangle**" command from the Sketch toolbar and draw the following sketch using two rectangles, starting at the origin and to the left (there will be two lines overlapping in the middle.) Don't be too concerned with their size; we'll add the correct dimensions later.

69. - It is a good practice to have single, non-intersecting profiles in the sketch, and no more than 2 lines sharing an endpoint. It is possible to use a sketch with intersecting lines using a function called "**Contours**", but that function is covered in the Level II book.

 As a general rule, it is always a good idea to work with single contour sketches, and advance to other techniques like Contours later on.

To clean up the sketch, we will use the "**Trim**" command from the Sketch toolbar, the lower left in the Mouse Gestures or the menu "**Tools, Sketch Tools, Trim**."

Trim Entities
Trims or extends a sketch entity to be coincident to another, or deletes a sketch entity.

70. - The Trim tool allows us to cut sketch entities using other geometric elements as a trim boundary. After selecting the "**Trim Entities**" icon, select the "Power Trim" option from the PropertyManager. The Power Trim allows us to click-and-drag *across* the entities that we want to trim. Click-and-drag the cursor crossing the two lines indicated next. Notice the lines are trimmed as you cross them.

END HERE

CLICK-AND-DRAG
STARTING HERE

71. - The next step is to extend the short line to close the sketch and have a single closed profile. Select the "**Extend Entities**" icon from the drop down menu under "**Trim Entities**" or if the "Trim Entities" is enabled, from the right-mouse-button menu. Click on the short line indicated; a preview will show you how the line will be extended. If the extension does not cross a line, you will not get a preview.

 Extend Entities can also be accessed with the right mouse button menu when using the **Trim Entities** command.

Another way to extend the line is to click-and-drag its endpoint onto other entities without selecting any tool.

72. - Add the following dimensions to the sketch using the "**Smart Dimension**" tool from the Sketch tab in the CommandManager or the Mouse Gestures.

73. - Now that the Sketch is fully defined we'll make the **Revolved Boss/Base**. Select "**Exit Sketch**" or the **Revolved Boss/Base** icon from the Features tab.

74. - The **Revolve** Property-Manager is presented and waits for us to select a line or centerline to make the revolved feature about it; if the sketch has a single centerline, it is selected automatically as a default axis of rotation. Select the line that we extended as the axis of rotation to make the revolved base.

75. - After selecting the line, notice the preview in the graphics area. The default setting for a revolved feature is for 360°. Click OK to complete the revolved feature and rename it "*Flange Base*."

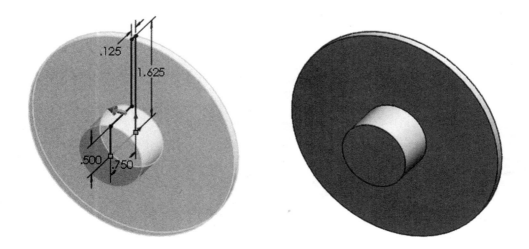

76. - Now switch to a Front view. We'll make a hole in the center of the cover for a shaft. Create a new sketch in the front most face of the cover (Small round face), or, select the small face and click in the "**Sketch**" icon from the pop-up toolbar. Draw a circle starting at the origin and dimension as indicated. Make a cut using the "**Extruded Cut**" command using the "Through All" option.

77. - The next step will be to make the first hole for the screws to pass through. We'll make one hole, and then use a Circular Pattern to make the rest as we did in the *'Housing'*, but in this case we'll use the **"Cut Extrude"** feature and not the **"Hole Wizard"** to show a different approach. To make this hole select the large circular face and create a new sketch. Draw a centerline from the origin toward the right, and at the end of the centerline draw a circle. Dimension as shown and make a cut using the "Through All" option as in the previous step.

 The centerline is used as reference geometry to locate the center of the circle. Optionally we can add a Horizontal relation between the circle's center and the origin to fully define it.

78. - A different way to do this sketch is to draw a circle and then convert it to construction geometry, this way you can dimension the circle's diameter. To convert any sketch element to construction geometry, simply select it in the graphics area and activate the "For construction" check box in the element's PropertyManager or click the "**Construction Geometry**" icon from the pop-up toolbar. Notice the circle is now displayed as construction geometry.

Now that the location circle is construction geometry (also known as *reference geometry*), draw the second circle for the hole making its center coincident with one of the quadrants of the reference circle as shown. Dimension the sketch and make the cut.

 An advantage of making the sketch using this technique is that you can add a diameter dimension to the circle locating the holes.

79. - To complete the rest of the holes, we'll make a circular pattern. Select the "**Circular Pattern**" icon from the Features tab in the CommandManager and select any circular edge for the pattern direction.

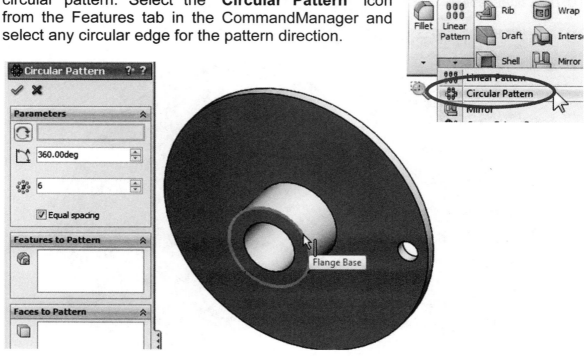

Now click inside the "Features to Pattern" selection box, and if not already selected, select the last cut operation from the fly-out FeatureManager or in the graphics area, using the "Magnifying Glass" (Shortcut "G") may help. Change the number of copies to 6; remember this count includes the original. Click OK to complete.

80. - Now select the Fillet command and round the edge as shown with a 0.125″ fillet radius.

81. - Edit the material for the part, and assign AISI-1020 steel. If it is not in the materials favorite list, select it from the library.

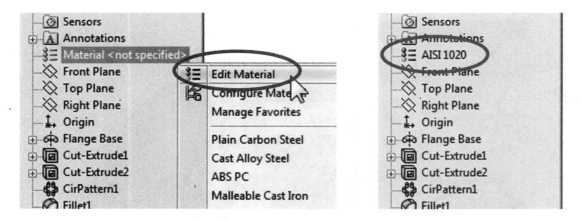

Save the finished component as *'Side Cover'* and close the file.

Exercises: Build the following parts using the knowledge acquired so far. Try to use the most efficient method to complete the model.

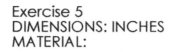

Exercise 5
DIMENSIONS: INCHES
MATERIAL:

Ø.250 (12X)   Ø.500 (12X)
Ø4.500   Ø2.000
A   A
.375
Ø6.000   Ø3.000
.625

.250   .250
1.000
.750
SECTION A-A
.250

HINT

.250   1.000
3.000
1.500   .750

M8x1.0 (8X)
21mm deep   A

30
12   12.500

A

75
12   45
12
R100
55

SECTION A-A

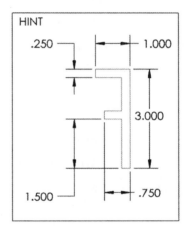

Exercise 6
DIMENSIONS: Millimeters
MATERIAL:

Engine Project Parts: Make the following components to build the engine. Save the parts using the name provided. High resolution images at mechanicad.com.

Ø1.095   Ø1.500

Ø.985

A — A

Ø1.200
Ø1.350

SECTION A-A

.240

R.040
.080

R.025

45°

.215

DETAIL B
SCALE 4 : 1

Oil Seal
DIMENSIONS: INCHES
MATERIAL:

Pin ConRod-Piston
DIMENSIONS: INCHES
MATERIAL: Alloy Steel

Ø.250   Ø.562

1.800

45°

.015

The Top Cover

Notes:

For the *'Top Cover'* part we will follow the next sequence of features. In this part we will learn a new feature called Shell, new options for Fillet and new end conditions for features (Boss, Cut, Revolve, etc.) Plus, we'll practice some of the previously learned features and options.

Base Extrude	Top Extrude	Corner cuts	Corner Fillet
Shell	Bottom Extrude	Top Fillet	Shell Fillet
Holes			

82. - We'll start by making a new document selecting the **Part** template from the "**New Document**" command, and just like we did with the *'Housing'*, we'll create a new sketch. Select the "**Extruded Boss**" command and then select the "*Top plane*."

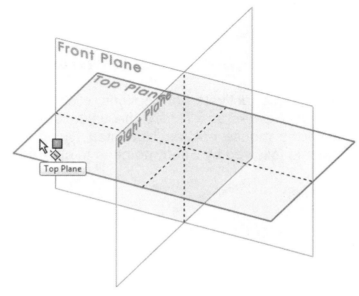

Draw a rectangle using the "**Center Rectangle**" command; first click in the origin to locate the center and then outside to complete the rectangle. Add the dimensions shown with the "**Smart Dimension**" tool and round the corners with the "**Sketch Fillet**" command using a 0.25″radius.

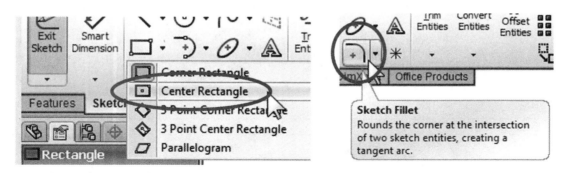

A slightly different way of making this (or any) sketch is by using the "**Sketch Numeric Input**." What this option does is to allow us to define geometry's exact size as we sketch, making it the correct size from the start. This option can be turned on in the menu "**Tools, Options, Sketch, Enable on screen numeric input on entity creation**", or the right mouse button menu. If using this option, it may be a good idea to also activate the "**Add Dimension**" option (this option is only available if a sketch tool is active.) The differences are:

Sketch Numeric Input allows the user to enter the exact size of geometry.
Add Dimension will add the dimensions to the geometry created.
Add Dimension is only available when *Sketch Numeric Input* is activated and a sketch drawing tool is selected, as seen in the following images.

To make the rectangle, activate both options, click to select the center of the rectangle *(do not click-and-drag.)* Notice the value boxes are immediately displayed as we move the mouse pointer. Now start typing the dimensions for each side of the rectangle followed by Enter, no need to click again.

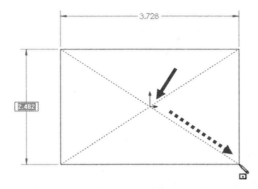

Click on center and move the mouse

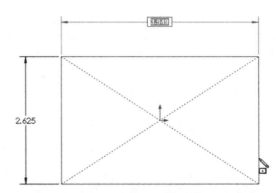

Type vertical dimension, press Enter

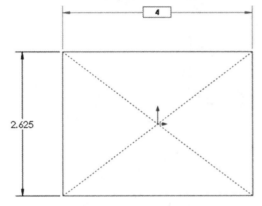

Type horizontal dimension, press Enter

Finished rectangle with dimensions

83. - To make the first extrusion, click on "**Exit Sketch**" and set the distance to 0.25″. Rename the extrusion *'Base'*.

84. -   For the second feature, we'll make an extrusion of similar shape to the first one, but smaller. For this feature we will use the "**Offset Entities**" function, this way the sketch will be created automatically by offsetting the edges of the previous feature face's edge. Click in the top face of the model and select the "**Sketch**" command from the pop-up toolbar to create a new sketch.

85. -   After creating the sketch, notice the top face of the first feature is selected (in highlighted color); while it is selected click the "**Offset Entities**" icon in the "Sketch" tab of the CommandManager. You will immediately see a preview of the offset of the face edges.

Mirror Entities

Offset Entities

Linear Sketch Pattern

Move Entities

Offset Entities
Adds sketch entities by offsetting faces, edges, curves, or sketch entities a specified distance.

86. - Change the offset value to 0.375″ and then click in the "Reverse" checkbox to make the offset inside, and not outside. Notice that when we change the direction the preview updates accordingly. Click OK when done.

87. - The Sketch is now Fully Defined (all geometry is black) because the sketch geometry is related to the edges of the face and only the offset dimension is added.

 Notice the offset command is powerful enough to eliminate the rounds in the corners if needed.

88. - To make the second feature select "**Extruded Boss**" from the Features toolbar in the CommandManager and extrude it 0.25″. Rename the feature *"Top Boss."*

89. - For the next feature, we'll make round cuts in the corners of the top extrusion to allow space for a screw head, washer and tools. Switch to a Top view and create a sketch in the topmost face. Make a circle as shown making sure the center is coincident to the corner. Feel free to use the Sketch Numeric Input in this sketch. Add two centerlines starting in the origin, one vertical and one horizontal; they'll be used in the next step. The model view was changed to Hidden Lines Removed for clarity.

The sketch grid can be turned on or off for better visualization, if needed, from the right mouse button menu.

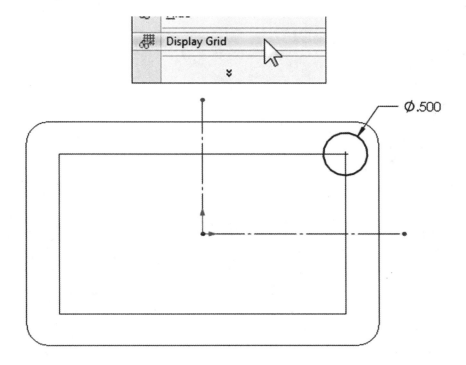

90. - We will now use the "**Mirror Entities**" from the Sketch tab in the CommandManager. This tool will help us make an exact copy of any sketch entity, in this case the circle, about any line, edge, or for our example, the vertical centerline; then we'll copy both circles about the horizontal centerline to make a total of four equal circles. Select the "**Mirror Entities**" icon.

91. - In the "Entities to Mirror" selection box select the circle. Then click inside the "Mirror About" selection box to activate it (it will be highlighted) and select the vertical centerline. Click OK to complete the first sketch mirror.

 In certain commands after making a selection, the mouse pointer will change to indicate us that pressing the Right Mouse Button will activate the next selection box or finish the command, helping us reduce mouse travel and work more efficiently. If we keep on selecting entities it has no effect and it will be dismissed.

92. - Now repeat the "**Mirror Entities**" command selecting both circles in the "Entities to Mirror" selection box, and using the Horizontal centerline in the "Mirror About" selection box. Click OK to finish the Mirror. Since the new circles are mirror copies of the original, and the original was fully defined, the sketch is therefore fully defined. The new circles are added a "Symmetric" relation about the centerline.

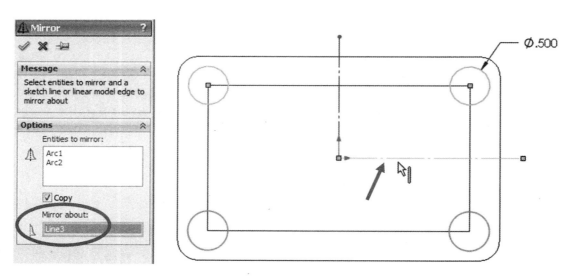

93. - We are now ready to make the cut. In this step we'll cut all four corners at the same time. SolidWorks allows us to have multiple closed contours in a sketch for one operation as long as they don't intersect or touch each other in one point. To add intelligence to our model (Design intent) we'll use an end condition for the cut called **Up to Surface**; with this end condition we can define the stopping face for the cut instead of giving it a size. Select the "**Extruded Cut**" icon, and select "Up To Surface" from the "Direction 1" options drop down selection box. A new selection box is activated; this is where we'll select the face where we want the cut to stop. Select the face indicated as the end condition and click OK to finish the feature.

The reason for selecting a face as an end condition is that if the height of the "Top Boss" changes, the cut will still go to the intended depth. This is the design intent and how we keep it by adding intelligence to our model.

Our part should now look like this:

94. - Using the "**Fillet**" command add a 0.25″ radius fillet to the edges indicated to round the corners. There are eight (8) edges to be rounded. To make selection easier, SolidWorks has a built in tool to help us select multiple edges. After selecting the first edge, a pop-up toolbar gives the user options to select different groups of edges. By moving the mouse over the different options highlights the edges that would be selected. For this example select the "Connected to end loop" option is exactly the edges we are interested in. In subsequent exercises the user will be able to explore other selection options.

After clicking in the icon to select the rest of the edges, the mouse changes to give us the OK in the right mouse button.

If selecting small edges is difficult, try using the "**Magnifying Glass**" to make selection easier (default shortcut "G".)

95. - Since this is going to be a cast part, we want to remove some material from the inside, and make its walls a constant thickness (common practice for castings and injection molded plastic parts.) The "**Shell**" command is the best tool for the job. The Shell creates a constant thickness part by removing one or more faces from the model. Select the "**Shell**" icon from the Features tab in the CommandManager. This is an applied feature, meaning that it does not require a sketch.

96. - In the Shell's PropertyManager under "Parameters" set the wall thickness to 0.125″ and select the face at the bottom of the part; this is the face that will be removed making every other face in the part 0.125″ thick. Click on OK to finish the command. Since we only have one shell feature in this part, there is no real need to rename it.

If no faces are selected the "**Shell**" command will create a hollow part.

97. - With the finished shell operation the part looks like this, with every face in the part 0.125″ thick.

How can we tell if the walls are really 0.125″ thick? Using the "**Measure**" tool. It is located under the Evaluate tab in the CommandManager. This tool is like a digital measuring tape, where we can select faces, edges, vertices, axes, planes, coordinate systems or sketch entities to measure to and from.

Activate the "**Measure**" tool and select the indicated face and edge; For better visibility expand the Measure box clicking in the double arrow icon. Notice the result in the Measure window as well as the tag (Dist .125in) in the graphics area giving the distance in all three X, Y and Z axes, as well as the normal distance between the selected entities. The dX, dY and dZ dimensions are measured distances between the points we selected. In this case we are interested in the dZ or the Normal Distance values, which are the same.

 To measure a different set of entities, click on an empty area of the graphics window, or make a right-mouse-click inside the selection box, and select "**Clear Selections**." This option works with every selection box.

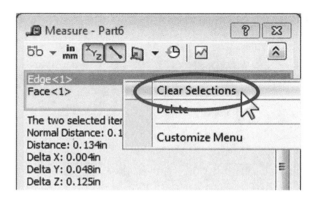

98. - To select a hidden face without having to rotate the component, make a right-mouse-click close to the face that we want to select, and use the "**Select Other**" command from the pop-up menu.

When we use the "Select Other" command, SolidWorks automatically hides the face we made a right-mouse-click on. Now we can see the faces behind it. When we touch them they are highlighted, and this way we know what we are selecting. We also get a list of faces behind the one removed where we can select the one we need. If we still cannot see the face we need, right-mouse-click other visible faces to hide them as needed. When we see the face we need, left-mouse-click to select it. Every hidden face will be made visible again after making a selection.

Right mouse button to hide face   Left mouse button to select hidden face

Select the hidden face indicated above, and then select the inner shell face. Feel free to make different measurements between Edge-Face, Edge-Vertex, Edge-Edge, Face-Vertex and Vertex-Vertex to see the results.

When we select a face first we are immediately presented with the area and perimeter of the selected face. Selecting a second face gives the distance between them plus the total area of both faces.

 In the "**Measure**" tool options, we can change the units of measure and precision if needed.

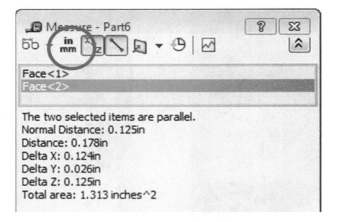

99. - The Shell operation left the outside corners thin and now we have to add material to reinforce them by adding an extrusion and have enough support for screws in the corners. Switch to a Bottom view (Ctrl+6) and create a sketch on the bottommost face as indicated and draw four circles concentric to the corner fillets. Do not worry about the size of the circles, we'll take care of that in the next step. Remember to touch the round edges to reveal their centers, and then draw the circle starting in the center to capture the concentric relation automatically.

100. - In order to maintain the design intent we are going to make the circles the same size as the corner fillets using an Equal geometric relation. Select the "**Add Relation**" icon from the Sketch Tab in the CommandManager or from the right mouse button pop-up menu.

Select all four circles and under "Add Relations", select **Equal** to make all circles the same size. Now that all circles are the same size, select one and make it either "Coradial" (same size and concentric) or "Equal" to the rounded corner to fully define the sketch.

101. - We will now make the extrusion using the "**Up to Surface**" end condition as we did in the last cut. Select the "**Extrude Boss/Base**" command from the Features tab, and use the option "**Up to Surface**." Select the face indicated as the end condition and select OK. By doing the extrusion this way we can be sure that our design will update as expected if any of the previous features changes.

Our part should now look like this:

102. - Add a 0.031″ radius fillet using the "**Fillet**" command from the Features tab. Select the two faces on top of the cover as indicated. Notice all the edges on the top side of the part are rounded with only two selections, maintaining our design intent and making our job easier at the same time.

103. - To add fillets to all the inside edges of the part we will use a slightly different approach. Instead of individually selecting the inside edges or faces, we will only select the "Shell1" feature from the fly-out FeatureManager, and add a 0.031″ radius. Adding the fillet using this technique will round every edge of the "Shell1" feature, making it much faster and convenient, not to mention that it maintains the design intent better.

 Selecting a feature to fillet as in this example can only be done using the fly-out FeatureManager or pre-selecting it in the FeatureManager before selecting the **"Fillet"** command.

Now every edge inside the part is rounded in one operation with only one selection.

104. - We are now ready to make four clearance holes for the #6-32 screws on the top. We'll use the **"Hole Wizard"** feature from the Features tab. Switch to a Top view for visibility and select the **"Hole Wizard"** icon.

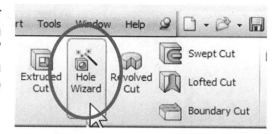

105. - In the first step of the **"Hole Wizard"**, select the "Hole" specification icon. From the "Type" drop down list select **"Screw Clearances."** From the "Size" selection list pick "# 6" and from "End Condition" select "Through All." This will create a hole big enough for a #6 size screw to pass freely through it.

106. - For the second step, click in the "Positions" tab and select the face indicated to add the hole's location sketch. After selecting the face, the **"Point"** tool is automatically selected and we are ready to add four points for the holes' centers. Touch the round corner edges to reveal their centers as we did in the *'Housing'* part, and click in one center to locate the hole. Repeat in the remaining corners to add all four holes.

Click OK to complete the "**Hole Wizard**."

107. - Change the part's material to "Cast Alloy Steel" as a final step. Save the part as *'Top Cover'* and close the file.

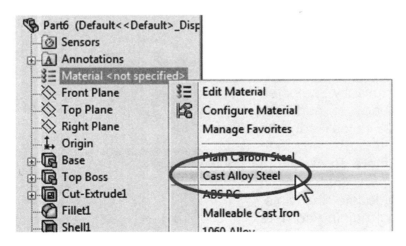

The finished part should look like this.

Exercises: Build the following parts using the knowledge acquired in this lesson. Try to use the most efficient method to complete the model.

Exercise 7
DIMENSIONS: INCHES
MATERIAL: AISI 1020

SECTION A-A

R.125

.750

1.000

SECTION A-A

Exercise 8
DIMENSIONS: INCHES
MATERIAL: ABS

.750

3.000

.625

.750

1.500

A

A

2.000

.500

R.500

.500

2.000

1.000

7.000

3.500

Engine Project Parts: Make the following components to build the engine. Save the parts using the name provided. High resolution images at mechanicad.com.

Oil Pan Gasket
DIMENSIONS: INCHES
MATERIAL:

Shaft Seal Cover
DIMENSIONS: INCHES
MATERIAL: Plain Carbon Steel

Shaft Seal Gasket
DIMENSIONS: INCHES
MATERIAL: VITON

The Offset Shaft

Notes:

For the *'Offset Shaft'* we'll follow the next sequence of operations. In this part we only need a few features. We'll learn how to make polygons in the sketch, a new option for the **"Cut Extrude"** feature, auxiliary planes and a Revolved cut.

Boss Extrude	Cut Revolve	Offset Plane
Second Cut	Hex cut	

108. - Start by making a new document selecting the Part template. For the first feature in this part create a sketch in the *"Right Plane."* A different way to create a sketch to how we've been doing it so far is to select the *"Right Plane"* in the FeatureManager, and from the pop-up toolbar select **"Sketch."**

The view will be oriented to the Right view automatically. Draw a circle starting at the origin and dimension it 0.600″ using the **"Smart Dimension"** tool. Since this shaft will need to meet certain tolerances for assembly, we will give a tolerance to the diameter.

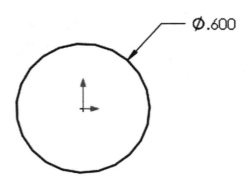

109. - To add (or change) the tolerance of the shaft's diameter, select the dimension in the graphics area. Notice the dimension's properties are displayed in the PropertyManager. This is where we can change the tolerance type. For this shaft select "Bilateral" from the "**Tolerance/Precision**" options box and add +0.000"/-0.005".

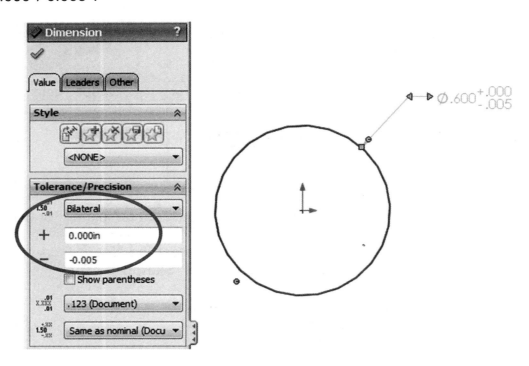

110. - When finished with the tolerance, extrude the shaft 6.5" using "**Extruded Boss/Base**" from the Features tab.

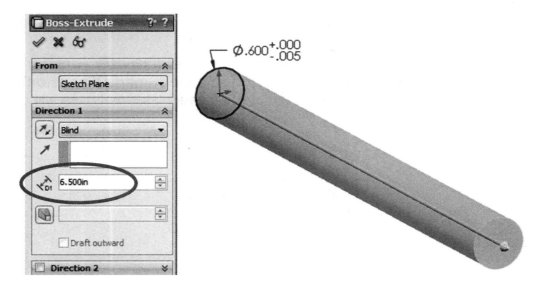

111. - For the second feature we'll make a "**Revolved Cut**." As its name implies, we'll remove material from the part similar to a turning (Lathe) operation. Switch to a Front view and select the "*Front Plane*" from the FeatureManager. From the pop-up menu select the "**Sketch**" icon as before to create a new sketch on it. Draw the following sketch and be sure to add the centerline. This is the profile that will be used as a "cutting tool." The centerline will be automatically selected as the axis of revolution for the cut.

 The reason for selecting the "*Front Plane*" for this sketch is because there are no flat faces to create the sketch in this orientation.

112. - Now that we are finished with the sketch, select the "**Revolved Cut**" icon from the Features toolbar.

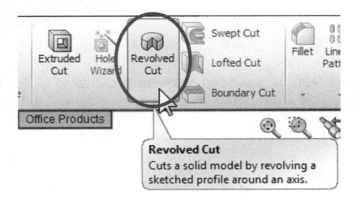

113. - Since we only have one centerline in the sketch, SolidWorks automatically selects it as the axis to make the revolved cut about it. By default a revolved cut is 360 degrees. Rotate the view to see the preview. Feel free to use the value spin box to change the number of degrees to cut, this will illustrate the effect of a revolve cut very clearly. Click OK to complete the feature and rename it *'Groove'*.

 If there is more than one centerline in the sketch, or none at all, we will be asked to select a line or model edge to use for the axis of revolution.

The part should now look like this.

114. - For the next feature, we need to make a cut exactly like the one we just did, but in the right side of the shaft. We could have done it at the same time with the previously made Revolved Cut feature, but we'll show a different way to make it and learn additional functionality at the same time.

For this feature, we'll create an auxiliary plane for a new sketch. Auxiliary Planes help us to locate a sketch where we don't have any flat faces or planes to use. To create an auxiliary plane select **"Reference Geometry**, **Plane"** from the Features tab in the CommandManager or from the menu **"Insert, Reference Geometry, Plane**." Planes can be defined using many different options using model vertices, edges, faces, sketch geometry, existing planes and/or axes.

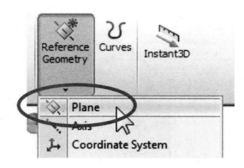

As we start selecting references to define a new plane, the possible ways to define it are dynamically shown in the PropertyManager, along with a preview of the plane in the graphics area. Some plane definitions require 1, 2 or 3 references depending on each case, but SolidWorks helps us by letting us know when the necessary options have been selected with a **"Fully Defined"** message at the top of the PropertyManager.

 Notice that references are color coded in the PropertyManager and matched in the graphics area to easily identify them.

Here are some of the most common ways to define an auxiliary plane:

Through Lines/Points – Select 3 non-collinear vertices, or one straight edge and one non-collinear vertex. Two or three references needed.

Parallel Plane at Point – Select an existing Plane or a flat face and a point. Note that when we select a Plane or flat face we get additional options like Parallel, Perpendicular, Coincident, at angle or distance. Two references are needed.

At an angle – Select a Plane or flat face and an Edge and enter the angle. The Plane's direction can be reversed using the "Flip" checkbox. In this case the face in the back was selected and the Edge indicated. The Edge acts as a "hinge" to the new plane. Change the angle using the value spin box to see the effect. Two references needed.

Offset Distance – Select a Plane or flat face, and define the distance from it to create the new Plane. "Flip" can be used to change the side on which the new plane is created. In this case the face in the back was selected and the new plane created to the right. We can optionally create multiple parallel planes changing the number of planes to create (default is 1.) One reference needed.

Normal to Curve – The plane is created by selecting an edge and a vertex of the edge. The plane created is perpendicular to the curve at the vertex. In this case we selected the edge and the vertex indicated. Two references needed.

On Surface – The plane is created selecting a surface (any surface) and a vertex (or sketch point/endpoint) on the surface. In this case the face is curved and the resulting plane is tangent to the face at the selected vertex. Two references are needed.

When creating auxiliary planes, we can use as references existing Planes, Faces, Vertices, sketch elements, Axes and Temporary Axes, the Origin, etc. To make sketch elements visible, expand a feature in the FeatureManager, select the sketch that we want to make visible, and from the pop-up toolbar select the **Show/Hide** icon. If the sketch is hidden, it will be made visible and vice versa.

115. - Back to our part, we'll make an Auxiliary Plane parallel to a face of the groove. Select "**Auxiliary Geometry, Plane**" from the Features tab. We'll make an auxiliary plane a set distance from the right face of the groove. Using the "**Select Other**" function (right mouse button menu or pop-up icon), select the indicated face below (hidden in this view.)

Notice the mouse pointer changes, letting us know that the left button is to select a face, and the right button to hide a face.

116. - Set the distance to 5″ and turn on the "Flip" checkbox if necessary. Notice the preview. After creating the plane, rename it to *"Offset Plane."*

 If the new plane is not visible, use the **"Hide/Show Items"** command. *"Front Plane"*, *"Top Plane"* and *"Right Plane"* are hidden by default; you can hide and show any plane the same way we did with the sketch.

117. - Switch to an Isometric view (for visibility) and select the *"Offset Plane"* in the graphics area; from the pop-up toolbar click on "**Sketch**" to create a new sketch on it.

The "**Convert Entities**" command is used to project existing geometric entities onto a sketch, such as model edges or other sketch entities and convert them to new sketch entities at the same time. Click on "**Convert Entities**" from the Sketch tab in the CommandManager, select the two edges indicated from the "*Groove*" feature and click OK to finish.

The two edges are projected onto the sketch plane and are automatically fully defined since they are a projected copy of the edges they came from adding an "On Edge" geometric relation; if the original groove changes, so will the converted entities. Make an "**Extruded Cut**" feature 0.063″ deep, going to the right. Rename the feature *"Offset Groove."*

118. - For the last feature, we'll add a hexagonal cut at the right end of the shaft. Hide the "*Offset Plane*" for easier visibility and switch to a Right view. Insert a sketch in the rightmost face of the shaft as indicated.

119. - We can make a polygon using lines, dimensions and geometric relations, but we really want to make it easy, so we'll use the "**Polygon**" tool. Go to the menu, "**Tools, Sketch Entities, Polygon**" or select the "**Polygon**" tool from the Sketch tab in the CommandManager.

 SolidWorks toolbars can be customized to add or remove icons as needed. Right-mouse-click on a toolbar, select "**Customize**" and from the "Commands" tab drag the commands needed to a toolbar.

120. - After we select the "**Polygon**" tool, we are presented with the options in the PropertyManager. This tool helps us to create a polygon by making it either inscribed or circumscribed to a circle. For this exercise we'll select the "Circumscribed circle" with 6 sides in the "Parameters" options. Don't worry too much about the rest of the options, as we'll fully define the hexagon using two additional geometric relations.

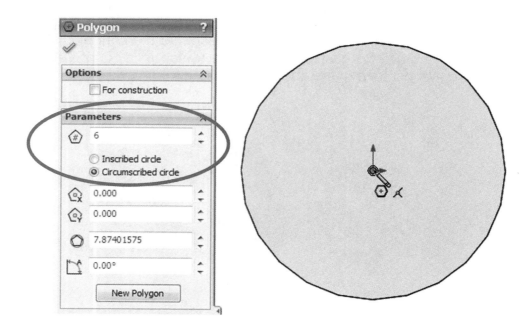

121. - Since the polygon is defined by a circle (Inscribed or Circumscribed), it is drawn like a circle. Start at the center of the shaft as shown and notice that we immediately get a preview of the hexagon, its radius and angle of rotation.

122. - Draw the circle a little smaller (or larger) than the shaft, the idea is to make the circumscribed construction circle the same size as the shaft using a geometric relation. Hit "Esc" or OK to finish the polygon tool when done.

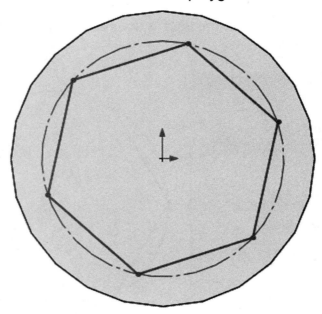

123. - Now select the "**Add Relation**" tool from the Sketch tab and select the polygon's construction circle and the edge of the shaft; add an "Equal" geometric relation to make them the same size.

 Remember that the "Add Relation" tool can also be found in the right mouse button menu.

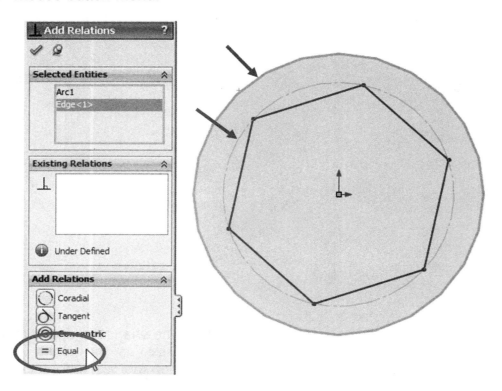

124. - Now select one of the hexagon's lines and add a "**Horizontal**" relation to fully define the sketch.

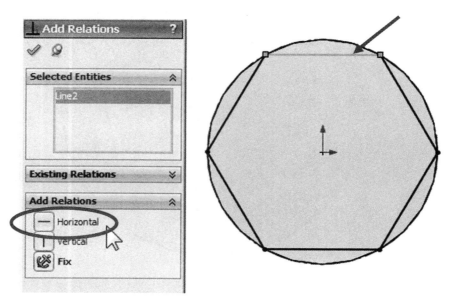

125. - Now we are ready to make the cut. For this operation we'll use a little used but very powerful option in SolidWorks. Select the **"Extruded Cut"** icon from the Features tab as before, but now activate the checkbox **"Flip side to cut."**

This option will make the cut *outside* of the sketch, not inside. Notice the arrow indicating which side of the sketch will be used to cut. Make the cut 0.5″ deep. Rename the feature *'Hex Cut'*.

126. - Edit the material for this shaft and select "Chrome Stainless Steel" from the materials library (or the Favorites list if available.)

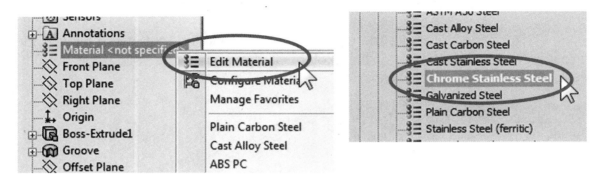

Save the part as *'Offset Shaft'* and close the file.

More about Auxiliary Geometry:

Auxiliary geometry includes **Planes**, **Axes,** **Coordinate Systems, Points, Mate References and Center of Mass.** Both of these can be created from the "**Reference Geometry**" icon in the Features tab in the CommandManager. Reference geometry can be used for a number of reasons, including locating features and components, as reference, or to use as part of a feature, an axis can be used to define the direction for a circular pattern and planes to add sketch geometry.

We covered the main options to create **Planes** previously, here are other types of Reference Geometry.

An **Axis** can be made using the following options:

One Line / Edge /Axis – Any linear edge, sketch line or axis. Every cylindrical and conical face has an axis (Temporary Axis) running through it. To reveal it use the menu "**View, Temporary Axis**."

Two Planes – An axis can be created at the intersection of any two planes.

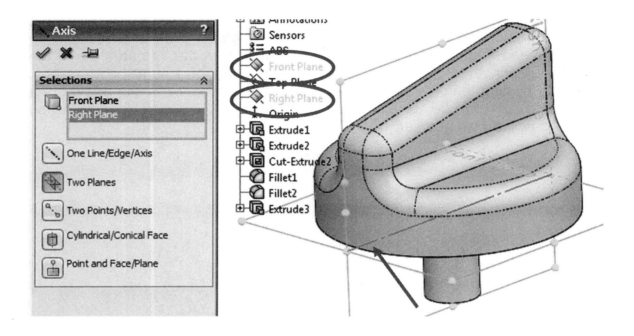

Two points/Vertices – Using any two vertices and/or sketch points/endpoints.

Cylindrical/Conical Face – Selecting any cylindrical or conical face will make an axis using the face's temporary axis.

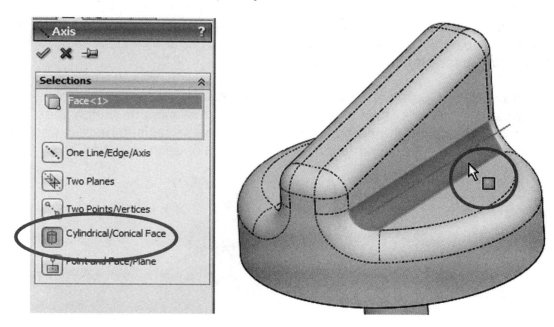

Point and Face/Plane – Selecting a point, sketch point or endpoint, or vertex and a flat face or plane will make an axis running perpendicular to the face/plane that passes through the point/vertex.

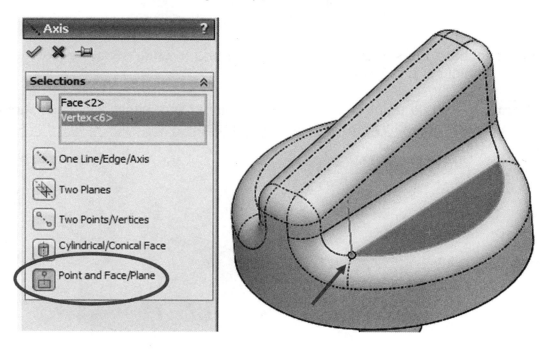

Coordinate Systems can be used for a number of things including to calculate a component's center of mass referenced to a specific location, or when we have to export parts for manufacturing on computer controlled machines using Computer Assisted Manufacturing (CAM). More often than not the origin the designer used for the component is not be the best location for the CAM operator to program the machining equipment.

To create a Coordinate System we need to select a vertex or point, and define two axis directions (X, Y or Z) using linear edges, axes or sketch lines; the third direction is defined automatically. Notice that an axis direction can be reversed using the "Reverse direction" icon to the left of each selection box.

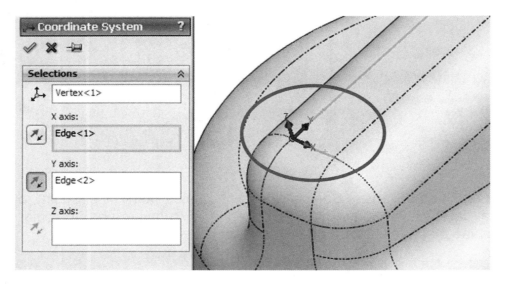

A Point can be added and used as a reference for other features, reference geometry, sketches, etc. Some

Arc Center – Adds a point in the center of a planar arc, either a circular model edge or a sketch arc. Only one reference is needed.

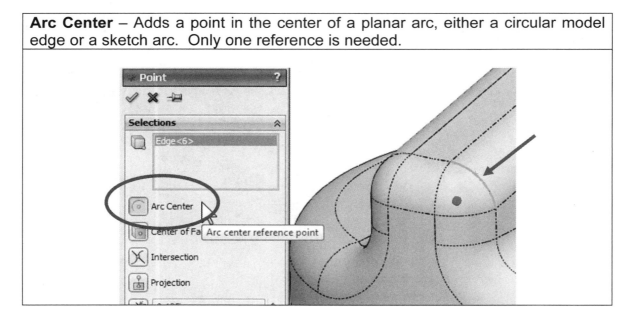

Center of Face – Creates a point at the center of mass of the selected face, either a planar or non-planar face. Only one reference is needed.

Intersection – Creates a point at the intersection of edges, curves or sketch segments. Two references are needed.

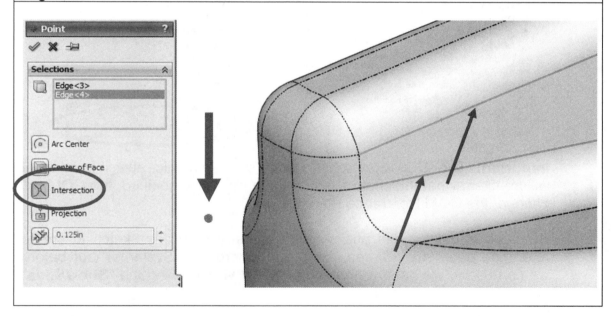

The **Center of Mass** (COM) adds a visual marker at the center of mass of the model, as well as a Center of Mass feature. After adding the COM we can add a **Center of Mass Reference Point** by right mouse clicking in the COM feature and selecting the COM Reference Point that can be used to dimension features from it.

Important: The "COM Reference Point" is not dynamic, after it is added it will be fixed; what this means is that if the model is modified, the COM *will change*, the COM Reference Point *will not*.

 Remember that we can use sketch geometry from any sketch to create reference geometry (Planes, Axes and Coordinate Systems), but before we can use it, we need to make the sketch visible using the "**Show/Hide**" button in the pop-up toolbar.

Exercises: Build the following parts using the knowledge acquired in this lesson. Try to use the most efficient method to complete the model.

Exercise 9
DIMENSIONS: INCHES
MATERIAL: 6061-T4 (SS)

 HINT: Draw a sketch with centerlines, exit the sketch and use it as a layout to make the auxiliary planes needed. Hide the layout sketch when finished.

Exercise 10
DIMENSIONS: INCHES
MATERIAL: 2024-O

4.000

3.000

Ø.625

Ø1.500

VIEW B-B

4X Ø .266 THRU ALL
⌴ Ø .438 ▼ .250

R.500

B

2.000

.750

45° B

2.000

.500

R.188
GROOVE

Engine Project Parts: Make the following components to build the engine. Save the parts using the name provided. High resolution images at mechanicad.com.

R.500

Ø .492 THRU ALL
M14X1.5 - 6H THRU ALL

Ø3.550

Ø5.500

.375

A

A

R.050

Ø3.000

Ø.750

B

.125

.125

SECTION A-A

.050

.750

R.350

DETAIL B
SCALE 1 : 1

Cylinder Head
DIMENSIONS: INCHES
MATERIAL: Cast Alloy Steel

Notes:

The Worm Gear

Notes:

For the *'Worm Gear'* we will make a simplified version of a gear without teeth. The intent of this book is not to go into gear design, but rather to help the user understand and learn how to use basic SolidWorks functionality. With this part we'll learn a new extrusion (or cut) end condition called "Mid Plane", how to chamfer the edges of a model, a special dimensioning technique to add a diameter dimension to a sketch used for a revolved feature, and how to add a dimension to a circle's perimeter. We'll also practice previously learned commands. For the *'Worm Gear'* we will follow the next sequence of features.

Mid Plane Extrusion	Revolved Cut 1	Revolved Cut 2	Mirror
Chamfer	Fillet	Keyway Cut	

127. - Start by making a new part document and create the following sketch in the *"Front Plane."*

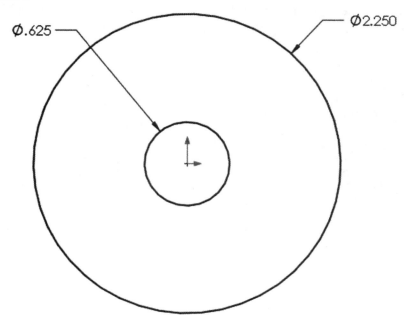

Ø.625

Ø2.250

128. - In this case we want the part to be symmetrical about the "*Front Plane*." To achieve this, we'll make an "**Extruded Boss/Base**" using the "**Mid Plane**" end condition; this condition extrudes half of the distance in one direction and half in the second direction. Change the end condition to "**Mid Plane**" and extrude it 1" (The result will be 0.5" going to the front and 0.5" going to the back.) Rename the feature "*Base*."

129. - For the second feature we will use a "**Revolved Cut**" to make the slot around the part. Change to a Right view select the "*Right Plane*" from the FeatureManager, and click on the "**Sketch**" icon from the pop-up toolbar as shown. Make the center of the circle coincident to the Midpoint of the cylinder's top edge and <u>don't forget the centerline</u>.

Ø.625

130. - Select "**Revolved Cut**" from the Features tab to complete the feature. Rename the feature *'Groove'*.

Ø.625

131. - Make a second revolved cut to remove material from one side. Switch to a Right view, and create a new sketch in the "*Right Plane*" as before using the following dimensions. Remember, it is a closed Sketch (four lines; don't forget the vertical line in the right side.) If needed, turn off the Sketch Grid and change to "Wireframe" view mode for clarity.

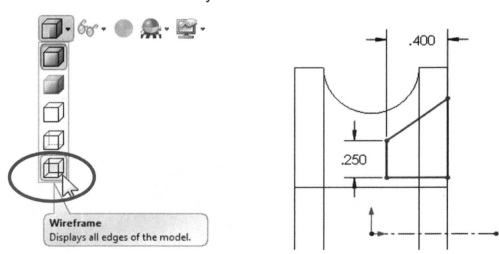

132. - We'll now use a new dimensioning technique to add diameter dimensions for Revolved Features, this way we will have a diameter dimension in the revolved feature when finished. Select the "**Smart Dimension**" tool, and add a dimension <u>from the Centerline</u> (not an endpoint!) to the top endpoint of the sketch. Before locating the dimension, cross the centerline and notice how the dimension value doubles. Locate the dimension, and change it to 2″. Immediately after adding the first dimension the Smart Dimension tool remains in Doubled dimension mode. Select the second horizontal line to add a 1″ dimension from the centerline.

133. - Make a "**Revolved Cut**" about the centerline to complete the feature. Notice the diameter dimensions; their purpose is more obvious in this image.

134. - Since the cut has to be on both sides of the part, to add the second cut we'll use the **"Mirror"** command to copy the previous **"Cut Revolve"** about the "*Front Plane*" as we've done before.

135. - To eliminate the sharp edges on the outside perimeter we'll add a 0.1″ x 45° **"Chamfer"**. The Chamfer is an applied feature similar to the Fillet, but instead of rounding an edge, it adds a bevel to it. Select it from the drop down menu under "Fillet" in the Features tab or in the menu **"Insert, Features, Chamfer."**

Set the options and values shown for the chamfer and select the two edges indicated. Click OK to finish.

136. - Add a 0.0625″ radius fillet to the four inside edges. Selecting the two faces inside will make selection easier.

137. - For the last step, we'll make the keyway. Switch to a Front view and make a sketch in the "*Front Plane*." Draw a rectangle and add a Midpoint relation between the bottom line and the origin.

We could have made the sketch in the front face, but we placed it in the "*Front Plane*" to show additional functionality.

138. - By adding the Midpoint relation, the rectangle will be coincident and centered with the origin. Add a 0.188″ width dimension as indicated. If the top horizontal line (blue) is below the center hole's circle, click-and-drag it until it's above the circle as shown. This will allow us to add a dimension to the circular edge.

139. - Now we need to add a dimension from <u>the top of the circular edge</u> to the horizontal line. Before adding the dimension, <u>press and hold</u> the "**Shift**" key, by doing this we'll be able to add the dimension from the top edge of the circle to the line of the rectangle; Select the circle at the topmost part of the circular edge and the line, click for the location and release the "**Shift**" key; change the dimension's value to 0.094″.

 If we don't hold the "**Shift**" key the dimension will be referenced to the circle's center instead.

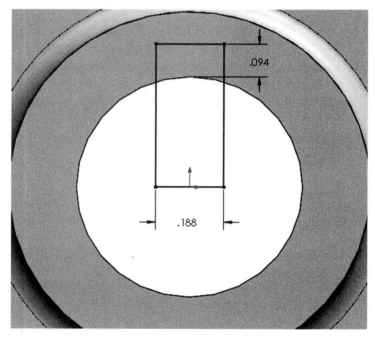

140. - To finish the part we need to make a Cut Extrude. Since the sketch is located in the "*Front Plane*" (in the middle of the part), making a cut "**Through All**" will only go from the center to one side. In this case we need to activate the "Direction 2" checkbox, and set the end condition to "**Through All**" for both "Direction 1" and "Direction 2."

 Notice the single and double arrows in the graphics area, indicating which one is Direction 1 and which is Direction 2. Any "End Condition" can be used for either direction as needed.

141. - Change the material to "AISI 1020" steel. Save the part as '*Worm Gear*' and close the file.

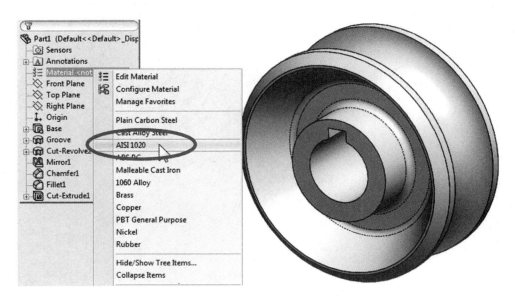

Exercises: Build the following part using the knowledge acquired in this lesson. Try to use the most efficient method to complete the model.

Exercise 11
DIMENSIONS: INCHES
MATERIAL:
Chrome Stainless Steel

Ø .201 THRU
1/4-20 UNC THRU

.500

A

A

.850

.525

R.200

Ø 2.250

.500

.750

SECTION A-A

.075 X 45°

1.500

4.000

Ø 4.000

Ø 6.000

Ø 3.000

1.250

Ø 2.000

6X Ø .201 THRU ALL
⌴ Ø .375 ▽ .190
(Counterbore for 10-32
Socket Head Cap Screw)

Ø 5.000

Engine Project Parts: Make the following components to build the engine. Save the parts using the name provided. High resolution images at mechanicad.com.

Bushing Top Con Rod
DIMENSIONS: INCHES
MATERIAL: Brass

$\emptyset.750\pm.002$ $\emptyset.563^{+.003}_{-.000}$

.500

.015 X 45°

Con Rod Crankshaft Half Bushing
DIMENSIONS: INCHES
MATERIAL: Brass

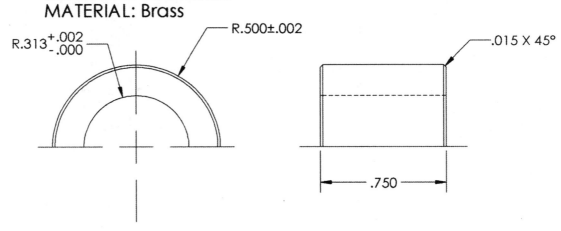

$R.313^{+.002}_{-.000}$ R.500±.002   .015 X 45°

.750

2.300

Connecting Rod
DIMENSIONS: INCHES
MATERIAL: 7075-O (SS)

2X ⌀ .213 THRU ALL
1/4-28 UNF THRU ALL

A

⌀1.125

⌀.750

.350
OFFSET

5.00°

⌀2.000

R.250

.500

A

R.500

.500

5.000

.250

.750

SECTION A-A

SECTION A-A

.125

.850

1.000

65°

.200

B

Crankshaft
DIMENSIONS: INCHES
MATERIAL: Alloy Steel

6.570

3.230

.480

2.200

A

A

.025 X 45°

R.025

R.125

.046

DETAIL B
SCALE 1 : 1

∅.940

∅1.000

∅.750

C

1.125

R.250

.300

C

∅1.135

R.750

∅.625

Ø.625

15°

R2.000

SECTION C-C

169

Notes:

The Worm Gear Shaft

Notes:

For the *'Worm Gear Shaft'* we will review the Revolved Feature previously learned, the sketch Polygon tool and a Mid Plane cut.

| Revolve | Keyway cut | Hex cut |

142. - In this part we only need to make three features. The first feature will be a revolved extrusion. Make a new part file and insert a sketch in the "*Front Plane*" as shown. It's very important to add the centerline, as we'll need it to add the diameter dimensions as we did in the previous part. Select the **"Revolved Boss"** command to complete the first feature. Rename the feature *'Base'*. Notice the three doubled diameter dimensions using the centerline.

 In a sketch like this is better to add the smaller dimensions before the larger ones. The reason is if the large dimensions are added first, when the geometry updates, the small features may behave unexpectedly.

Add a "Collinear" relation between the two lines indicated before dimensioning.

143. - The second feature is the keyway. Select the "*Front Plane*" from the FeatureManager and click in the "**Sketch**" icon from the pop-up toolbar. In this sketch it's OK to leave the top line of the sketch under defined. What we'll do is make a cut using the "**Mid Plane**" end condition. The top line beyond the top of the part allows us to "cut air"; this way we are sure we will cut the part. This is a common practice and is fine as long as we make sure the sketch is big enough to accommodate possible future changes. Adding a small dimension to ensure the sketch extends past the part is usually a good idea too.

 Remember that we can use Mouse Gestures (right mouse click-and-drag) for the most commonly used commands, or configure it for the tools we use most to help us speed up the design process.

An useful option when drawing lines, is to transition from drawing a line to a tangent arc. To do this we can use the default shortcut key "A" or move the mouse back to the last endpoint. After moving the mouse back, a tangent arc will be started. Depending on the direction that we move out, that's the direction the tangent arc will be created. Select the "**Line**" tool and draw a line, then click in one location, click in the second point to complete the first line, and instead of clicking a third time to add a second line, move back to the second endpoint and move out to add a tangent arc. Press "A" to toggle between arc and line.

First click…	second click…	move out (*or* press A)…
	0.59, 180°	*0.4*
back to second point…	and out going up…	or out going down…
	A =	*A = 5:*
…or straight up…	…or straight down…	…or back.
A = 53.	*A = 75.01°*	*A = 90° R = 0.*

The 0.250" dimension's only purpose is to make sure the sketch cuts through the part by extending the sketch a little beyond the part. To avoid importing this dimension to the detail drawing later on, right mouse click on the dimension it and uncheck the "Mark for Drawing" option.

144. - Select the "**Cut Extrude**" command from the Features tab and use the "**Mid Plane**" end condition with a dimension of 0.1875"; this way the keyway will be exactly at the center of the shaft. Notice that the "Direction 2" option box is unavailable when we select the Mid Plane end condition.

145. - For the last feature we'll make a hexagonal cut just as we did in the *'Offset Shaft'*. Switch to a Left view, select the leftmost face and create a sketch. Using the "**Polygon**" tool from the Sketch tab draw a Circumscribed hexagon and make the construction circle equal to the shaft's end.

Polygon
Sketches a polygon. You can change the number of sides after sketching the polygon.

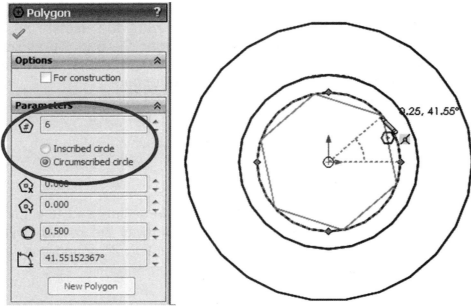

Finally make one line horizontal to fully define the sketch.

146. - Make a "**Cut Extrude**" using the "Up to Surface" end condition as indicated and activate the option "Flip side to cut" to cut *outside* the hexagon.

147. - Change the material to "Chrome Stainless Steel." Feel free to add the most commonly used materials using the "**Manage Favorites**" option.

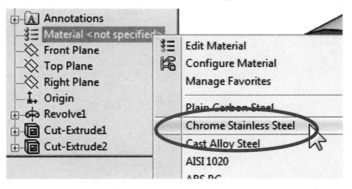

148. - Save the part as *'Worm Gear Shaft'* and close the file.

Engine Project Parts: Make the following components to build the engine. Save the parts using the name provided. High resolution images at mechanicad.com.

The following part is shown in three steps for clarity

Sealed Needle Bearing
DIMENSIONS: INCHES
MATERIAL:

Ø1.250
Ø1.500

.100
.500

Ø1.300

.015 X 45°
SECTION A-A

Ø.155
20 INSTANCES

Ø1.000

.400

SECTION A-A

Ø1.000

.400

.040

SECTION A-A

Internal Retaining Ring
DIMENSIONS: INCHES
MATERIAL: Alloy Steel

Retaining Ring Crankshaft Bearing
DIMENSIONS: INCHES
MATERIAL: Alloy Steel

DETAIL A
SCALE 4 : 1

A help sheet with a sequence of features is located in the Appendix for this part.

DETAIL D
SCALE 1 : 1

DETAIL C
SCALE 1 : 1

SECTION B-B

SECTION A-A

Piston Head
DIMENSIONS: INCHES
MATERIAL: 6063-O

Special Features: Sweep, Loft and Wrap

There are times when we need to design components that cannot be easily defined by prismatic shapes. For those features that have 'curvy' shapes we can use **Sweep** and **Loft** features, which let us create almost any shape we can think of. These are the features that allow us to design consumer products, which, more often than not, have to be attractive and appealing, making extensive use of curvature and organic shapes. These products include things like your remote control, a computer mouse, coffee maker, perfume bottles, telephones, etc., and many times the success or failure of these products in the market can be directly attributed to their appearance. They have to look nice, 'feel' right, and of course perform the task that they were intended for. Sweeps and Lofts are also prevalent in the automotive and aerospace industry where cosmetics, aerodynamics and ergonomics are a very important part of the design process.

Sweeps and Lofts have many different options that allow us to create from simple to extremely complex shapes. In light of the vast number of variations and possibilities for these features, we'll keep these examples as simple as possible without sacrificing functionality, to give the reader a good idea as to what can be achieved.

Sweeps and Lofts are usually referred to as advanced features, since they usually require more work to complete, and a better understanding of the basic concepts of solid modeling. Having said that, these exercises will assume that any command that we have done more than a couple of times up to this point, like creating a sketch, are already understood and we'll simply direct the reader to create it providing the necessary details. This way we'll be able to focus more on the specifics of the new features.

The Wrap feature is a special tool that helps us, as the name implies, to 'wrap' a sketch around a surface, this tool helps us create features like cylindrical cams, slots on cylinders or cylindrical surfaces, etc.

These are some examples of designs made with advanced modeling techniques.

Sweep: Cup and Springs

Notes:

For this exercise we are going to make a simple cup. In this exercise we will learn a new option when creating features called "**Thin Feature**", the Sweep feature, a new Fillet option to create a Full Round fillet, and a review of auxiliary Planes. The sequence of features to complete the cup is:

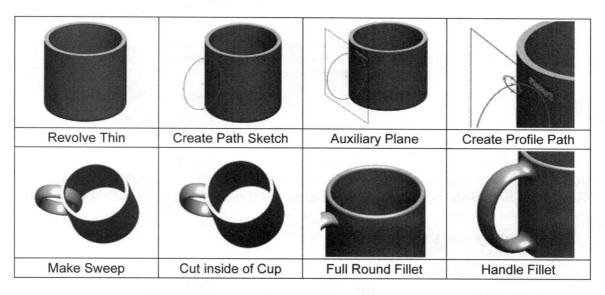

Revolve Thin	Create Path Sketch	Auxiliary Plane	Create Profile Path
Make Sweep	Cut inside of Cup	Full Round Fillet	Handle Fillet

149. – For the first feature we will create a "**Revolved Feature**" using the "Thin Feature" option. This option makes a feature with a specified thickness based on the sketch that was drawn. Select the "*Front Plane*" and create the following sketch. Notice the sketch is an open profile with two lines, an arc and a centerline. (Remember to make the diameter dimension about the centerline.)

150. - After selecting the "**Revolve Boss/Base**" command we get a warning telling us about the sketch being open. Since we want a thin revolved feature, select "No."

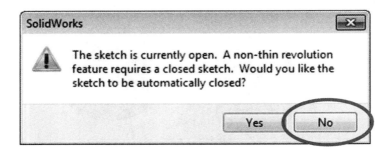

In the "Revolve" options, "**Thin Feature**" is automatically activated. Since we want the dimensions we added to be external dimensions, select the "**Reverse Direction**" option to add the material inside the cup. Notice the preview showing the change.

 In the value box we typed 3/16; we can add a fraction and SolidWorks changes it to the corresponding decimal value when we click OK. We can also type simple mathematic expressions including addition, subtraction, multiplication and division in any value box where we can type a value.

Our thin feature now looks like this:

151. - Select the "*Front Plane*" and create the following sketch using an ellipse. Be sure to add a "Vertical" geometric relation between the top and bottom points of the ellipse to fully define it. Select the "**Ellipse**" command from the Sketch tab in the CommandManager or from the menu "**Tools, Sketch Entities, Ellipse**." Add the corresponding dimensions to and from the ellipse points at the major and minor axes. To draw an ellipse select the center point, then one axis and then the other axis.

Exit the sketch and rename it *"Path."* We will not use the sketch for a feature just yet.

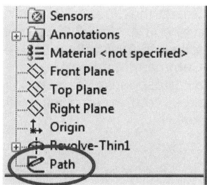

152. - Create an Auxiliary plane parallel to the "*Right Plane*" using the center of the ellipse as a second reference as shown.

153. - Select the plane just created and draw the next sketch. Start the center of the new ellipse at the top point of the previous sketch's ellipse. Add a coincident relation if needed. Remember to add a horizontal relation between the points of the major (or vertical to the minor) axis. Exit the sketch and rename it *"Profile."*

154. - Select the "**Sweep**" icon from the Features tab in the CommandManager. The sweep is a feature that requires a minimum of two sketches: one for the sweep profile and one for the path (the path can also be a model edge or a user defined curve.)

In the "**Sweep**" properties, select the *"Profile"* sketch in the Profile selection box, and the *"Path"* sketch in the Path selection box. Optionally, a Sweep can have guide curves and other parameters to better control the resulting shape, but in this case we are using only the basic options. Notice the preview and click OK when done. Hide the auxiliary planes using the "**Hide/Show Items**" toolbar if so desired.

155. - Notice the sweep is also inside the cup. We will make a cut to fix this. Create a sketch in the flat face at the top of the cup. Select the <u>inside</u> edge at the top and use "**Convert Entities**" from the Sketch tab to convert the edge to sketch geometry. Select the "**Extruded Cut**" icon and use the "Up to next" end condition from the drop down selection list. This end condition will make the cut until it finds the next face (the bottom) effectively cutting the part of the handle inside the cup.

156. - Now we need to round the flat face at the top lip of the cup. To do this we'll add a "**Fillet**" using the "**Full Round Fillet**" option. The full round will essentially remove the flat face at the top, and replace it with a rounded face.

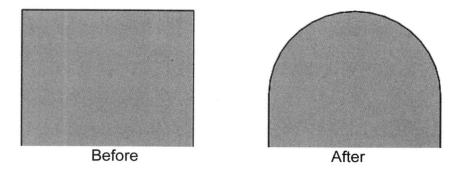

Before   After

We need to select three faces, the middle face will be the one replaced by the fillet. After selecting the Fillet command, select the "Full round fillet" option to reveal the selection boxes. With the first selection box active select the outside face of the cup. Click inside the second selection box and select the top flat face of the cup. Click inside the third selection box and select the inside face of the cup. Note the selected faces are color coded. When done selecting faces click OK to apply the fillet.

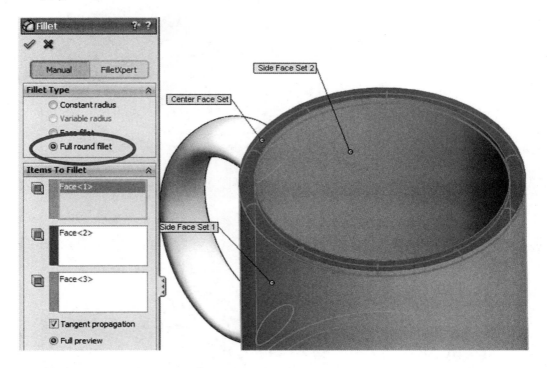

157. - To finish the cup add a fillet to round the edges where the handle meets the cup. Select the fillet command with the "Constant Radius" option, select the handle's surface and change the radius to 0.25". Click OK to finish.

158. - Save the finished part as *'Cup'* and close.

In the next exercise we are going to show how to make a simple and a variable pitch spring. In order to make these springs we'll have to learn how to make simple and variable pitch helixes to be used for the sweep paths. The sequence of features to complete the springs are:

Simple Spring

Draw circle	Make Helix	Draw Spring Profile Sketch	Make Sweep

Variable Pitch Spring

Draw circle	Make Variable Pitch Helix	Make Spring Profile sketch	Make Sweep and cut ends

Simple Spring

159. - In order to make a helix, first we need to make a sketch with a circle. This circle is going to be the helix's diameter. Select the "*Front Plane*" and make a sketch using the following dimensions. Exit the sketch when done.

 If we don't exit the sketch, we'll only have the "Helix and Spiral" option from the "Curves" command.

160. - In the Features tab select "**Curves, Helix and Spiral**" from the drop-down icon or the menu "**Insert, Curve, Helix/Spiral**." If asked to select a plane or a sketch, select the sketch we just drew.

 If we select the "**Helix and Spiral**" command before exiting the sketch, SolidWorks will use that sketch automatically for the helix.

161. - The helix can be defined by the combination of any two parameters between Pitch, Revolutions and Height and the third parameter is calculated.

For this example we'll select "Pitch and Revolution" from the "Defined By:" drop down menu, and make the pitch 0.325" and 6 Revolutions. The "Start Angle" value defines where the helix will start. By making it 90 degrees it will start at the top, coincident with the "*Front Plane*." If we had made it 0 degrees, it would be coincident to the "*Top Plane*" instead (Feel free to explore the options.)

 Note the Helix command has options to make it Counterclockwise, Clockwise, Tapered, Variable pitch and reversed (going right or left.)

162. - Once the Helix is done, we need to make the profile sketch for the sweep. Switch to a Right view, and add a new sketch in the "*Right Plane*" as shown. Make the circle close to the Helix...

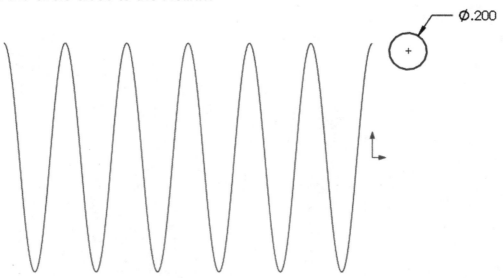

... and add a "**Pierce**" geometric relation between the center of the circle and the helix. This way the path will start at the beginning of the helix. This relation will make the sketch fully defined. Exit the Sketch when done.

 A pierce relation is done between an element that is oblique or perpendicular to the sketch plane and a point in the sketch. Think of it as a needle piercing through a fabric, the sketch being the fabric and the helix (or curve, model edge or another sketch) the needle.

163. - Select the Sweep command and make the sweep using the last sketch as a profile and the Helix as a Path. Note the Preview and click OK to finish.

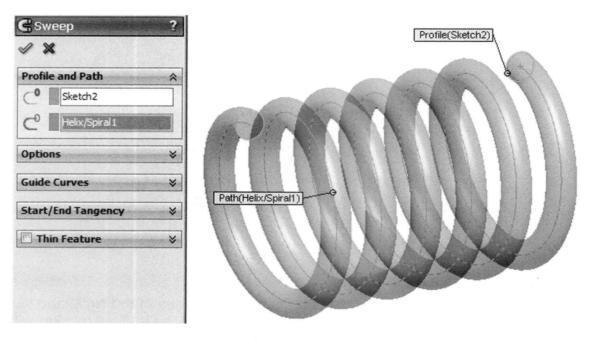

Save as '*Spring*' and close the finished spring.

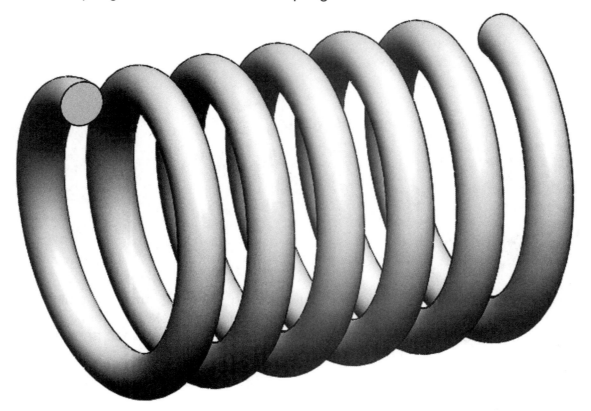

Variable Pitch Spring

164. - For the variable pitch spring we'll start the same way and make the following sketch in the "*Front Plane*." This will be the spring's outside diameter.

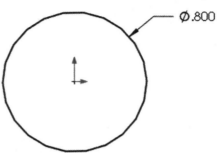

165. - While still editing the sketch, in the Features tab from the "**Curves**" drop down icon select "**Helix and Spiral**"; notice it is the only option available.

166. - In the **Helix/Spiral** command select "Pitch and Revolution" from the "Defined by:" selection box and "Variable Pitch" in the Parameters box. After selecting it we are presented with a table, fill in the values for the helix with the following values. Click OK when finished to build the helix.

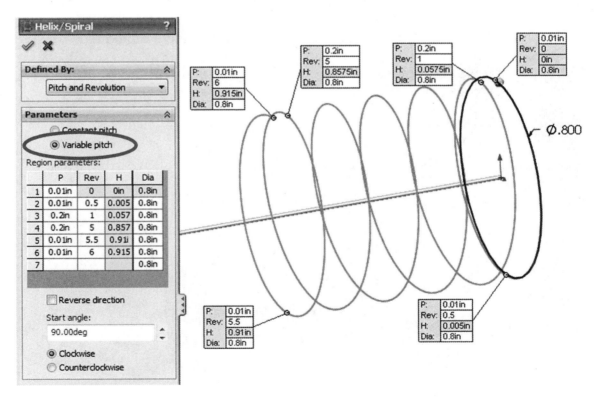

167. - After the helix is complete add a new sketch in the "*Right Plane*." Draw the circle first, then add a center rectangle; trim and dimension as needed.

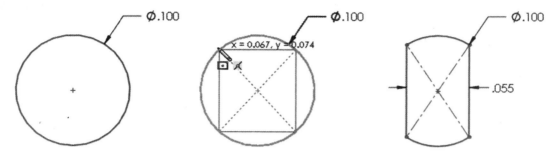

168. - Add a centerline from the center to the top line (make sure it is coincident.) Select the endpoint of the centerline and the helix to add a "**Pierce**" geometric relation to make the sketch fully defined.   Exit the sketch and optionally rename it *'Profile'*.

The Pierce relation allows us to fix the profile to the path, and can be added to any part of the sketch. We chose to add it to the top because the original sketch used for the helix is the spring's outside diameter.

169. - Just as we did before, select the "**Sweep**" command, add the path and profile as shown and click OK to finish.

---

170. – To finish we'll make a cut to flatten the sides of the spring. Change to a Right view and add a sketch in the "*Right Plane*." Draw a single line starting at the midpoint of the indicated edge and long enough to cross the part.

171. - Select the "**Extruded Cut**" command. When we use an open sketch to make a cut, the "Through All" option is automatically selected in both directions. One side of the model is cut using the open sketch. The small arrow located at the center of the line indicates which side of the model will be cut. Use the "Flip side to cut" option to cut the left side, otherwise the biggest part of the spring will be cut. Click OK to complete the cut extrude and repeat it in the right side. Note the cutting plane is shown in the graphics area.

 When using an open sketch to cut a model, we can only use a single open profile. If we have multiple open profiles we cannot make the Cut Extrude.

Save the model as *'Variable Pitch Spring'*.

A note about threads

Threads can be added to a model either by adding a Sweep or a Cut Sweep with a helix. When modeling screws and fasteners in general, it is almost always unnecessary to add a helical thread, as it consumes a large amount of computing resources, and a simple representation of it usually suffices (as a Revolved Boss/Cut or Cosmetic Thread.) It is strongly advised to only add threads when required by the model, as in the following bottle exercise.

For the next exercise we'll build the following bottle using a sweep feature with guide curves.

This bottle will be made using a Sweep feature for the body and one for the thread. For the body we'll make a sweep with two guide curves, so we need to make four sketches: Path, Guide Curve 1, Guide Curve 2 and Profile, in that order. The reason to make the Profile last is that it has to pierce the Path and both Guide Curves.

172. - Open a new part, set dimensions to inches and three decimal places. Make the Path sketch in the "*Front Plane*" and Exit the sketch. Rename *'Path'*.

173. - Add a second sketch in the "*Front Plane*." Make arcs and lines tangent to each other, add centerlines as reference for tangency. All arcs are equal. Exit sketch and rename *'Guide 1'*.

174. - Add third sketch to "*Right Plane*." Add geometric relations to previous sketches to maintain design intent. Make the topmost endpoint Horizontal to the topmost endpoint of the '*Path*' sketch. Arcs are equal size and tangent. Make the indicated endpoints horizontal. Only geometric relations and two dimensions are needed to fully define the sketch. Exit the sketch and rename it '*Guide 2*'.

Right view   *View between front and right*

175. - Add a new sketch in the "*Top Plane*", make an ellipse adding Pierce relations between the ellipse's major and minor axes to '*Guide 1*' and '*Guide 2*'. Exit the sketch and rename it *'Profile'*.

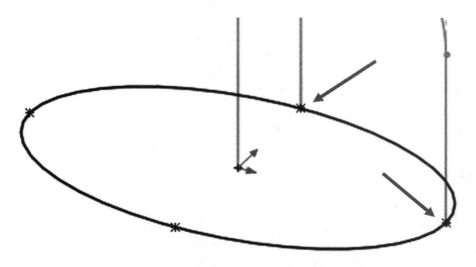

176. - Select the "**Sweep Boss/Base**" icon, add the *'Path'* sketch to the "Path" selection box and the *'Profile'* sketch to the "Profile" selection box. Expand the "Guide Curves" selection box and add both guides to it. Click OK to finish.

177. - Add a sketch on the top face using "Convert Entities" and extrude it 1".

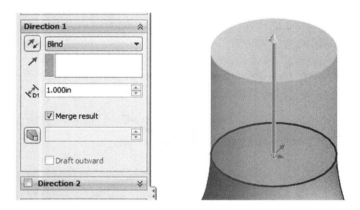

178. - Add a 0.375" fillet at the bottom of the bottle.

179. - Add a 0.050" shell to the part, remove the top face.

180. - Add auxiliary plane parallel to the topmost face 0.125" below it.

181. - Add sketch to this plane, use Convert Entities to project top outside edge, and make a Helix with a 0.2" pitch, 2.5 turns. Start helix at 0 degrees.

182. - Add the following sketch to the "*Right Plane*." Be sure to add a Pierce relation between the profile and the helix. Exit the sketch and make a sweep feature using the helix and this profile.

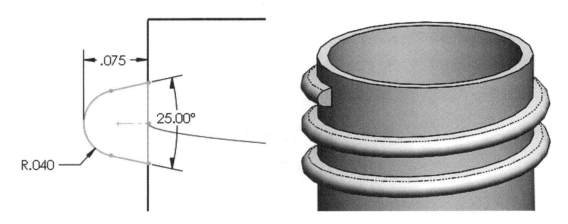

183. - Add a sketch on the front face of the thread, use Convert Entities and make a 120 degrees "Revolved Boss." Add a second one at the other end of the thread.

184. - Add a 0.02" fillet to the thread as a finishing touch. You may need to select multiple edges.

Engine Project Parts: Make the following components to build the engine. Save the parts using the name provided. High resolution images at mechanicad.com.

Intake
DIMENSIONS: INCHES
MATERIAL: Chrome Stainless Steel

Ø1.000

.035

Ø.750

R.125

.115

1.500

R1.000

.250

1.500

R.250

4X Ø .266 THRU ALL

1.000

1.500

1.250

1.750

Ø.450

R.010   .035

THREAD PROFILE
PITCH: 0.075"
TURNS: 3

.075

.038
.025

.028

DETAIL B
SCALE 4 : 1

A

R.025

.250

.150

FULL RADIUS

B

4.000

90°   .250

R.025

5.000

45°

.025

SECTION A-A

Oil Dip Stick
DIMENSIONS: INCHES
MATERIAL:

Loft: Bottle

Notes:

The "**Loft**" feature requires at least two different sketches and/or faces and optionally guide curves to more accurately define the final shape. The **Loft** helps us design complex shapes with more control over the cross section. In this exercise we will make a bottle using a loft with four different sketches.

185. - Make a new part and create three auxiliary planes using the "**Plane**" command. Select the *"Top Plane"* as reference, change the number of planes to 3 and space them 2.5″ as shown. Click OK when done.

186. - For clarity, select the *"Top Plane"* in the FeatureManager and show it using the "Hide/Show" command from the pop-up toolbar.

187. - Switch to a Top view, select the *"Top Plane"* and draw the following sketch using the "**Center Rectangle**" and "**Sketch Fillet**" tools. Exit the sketch when finished.

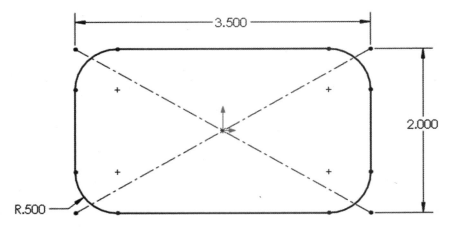

188. - Still in the Top view, select *'Plane1'* from the FeatureManager and create the second sketch. Use the "**Center Rectangle**" tool; be sure to start in the origin and make the rectangle's corner coincident to the previous sketch's diagonal line. Add a 2.5″ width dimension and the 0.5″ "**Sketch Fillet**" to fully define the sketch. Exit the second sketch when finished.

 Turn off the display of Planes for clarity with "Hide/Show Items."

189. - For the third profile, select *'Plane2'* from the FeatureManager and create a new sketch in it. This sketch will be exactly the same as the first one. To help us save time and maintain design intent, we'll use the "**Convert Entities**" tool. In the "**Convert Entities**" selection box, select the entire *Sketch1* from the fly-out FeatureManager and click OK to project Sketch1 in the new sketch. Exit the sketch when done.

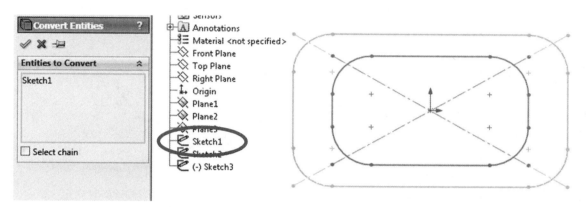

190. - For the last profile select *'Plane3'* from the FeatureManager and create a new sketch. Draw a circle and add a geometric relation to make it "Tangent" to the horizontal line in *'Sketch2'* as indicated. This relation will fully define the sketch. Exit the sketch to finish.

 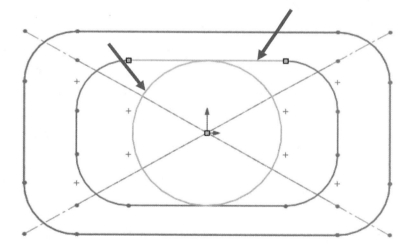

191. - The finished sketches will look like this with the planes visible:

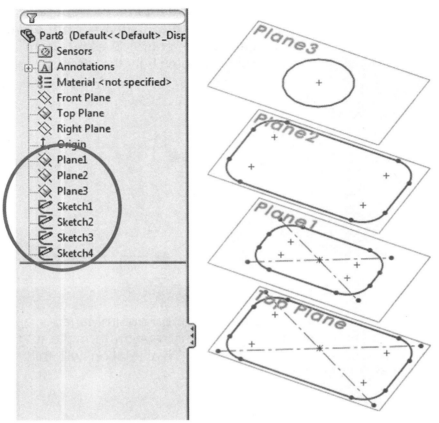

192. - Now we are ready, select the "**Loft**" icon from the Features tab. The loft feature requires two or more sketches and/or faces, and we'll use the four sketches we just made to build the bottle.

We will select the profiles starting with the first one we made at the bottom and finishing with the last one at the top. It is important to select the sketches thinking that where we select the profile will affect the result. Click in the graphics area near the indicated 'dots', this line indicates the segment of one profile that will be connected to the next profile. If we select points randomly in the profiles, the loft could twist and produce undesirable results. Optionally, guide curves can be added to improve control of the resulting shape.

From the "Start/End Conditions" select "Normal to Profile" for both the "Start" and "End" constraint. Notice the difference in the preview after selecting the start and end constraints. Click OK when done.

193. - Add a 0.25″ radius fillet in the bottom edge of the part to round it off.

Finish the part using the "Shell" tool; select the top face to remove it and make the wall thickness 0.125".

Image shown using Real View

194. - To view the inside of the part, select the "**Section View**" icon from the View toolbar or the menu "**View, Display, Section View.**" We can define which plane to cut the model with, the depth of the cut and optionally add a second or third section. If we click OK in the Section View, the model will be displayed as cut, but this is only for display purposes; the part is not actually cut. To turn off the Section View, select its icon or menu command again. This section view can be used along with the "**Measure**" tool to inspect the part.

Section View
Displays a cutaway of a part or assembly using one or more cross section planes.

 We can also change the depth of the cut by dragging the arrow in the center of the plane.

Save the part as '*Bottle Loft*' and close.

Wrap Feature

The wrap feature helps us create cylindrical cams or slots on cylindrical surfaces using a sketch on a plane tangent to the surface we want to make the wrap on.

195. – Make a new part, set units to inches with three decimal places; add this sketch on the *"Front Plane"* and extrude it 3".

196. – The next step is to make the sketch that will be used for the wrap feature. For the sketch plane we have an option of using the *"Top Plane"*, *"Right Plane"* or create a new plane tangent to the cylinder's surface. For this example we'll use the *"Top Plane."* Draw the following profile first making sure its symmetrical about the centerline. All arcs are equal radii. The top dimension's value is entered as **1.5 * pi**, since we want the sketch to wrap completely around the cylinder. SolidWorks automatically calculates the resulting value for us.

197. - The sketch so far is the centerline of the slot we are going to wrap around the cylinder. Select the "**Offset**" command and turn on the options:
"**Select chain**" to automatically select the entire centerline picking only one segment, "**Bi-directional**" to make the offset in both directions, "**Make base construction**" to make the selected line (or chain) construction geometry, and after selecting a segment of the sketch the "**Cap ends**" option is enabled letting us choose to cap the offset with Arcs or Lines. Making the offset 0.25" will give us a 0.5" wide slot. Click OK to complete the offset and exit the sketch. Note how the original sketch is now construction geometry and we have a closed profile. Exit the sketch when done.

198.- Select the "**Wrap**" feature from the Features tab or the menu "**Insert, Features, Wrap**." If the sketch is not pre-selected, select the sketch from the graphics area.

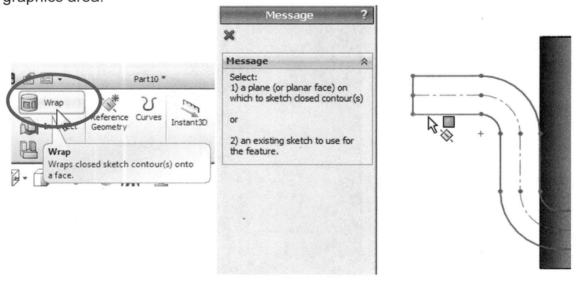

199.- Select the "Deboss" option to make a cut in the part (The "Emboss" option will add material and the "Scribe" will split the face.) Select the cylinder's face in the "Face for Wrap Feature" selection box and make the depth 0.1". Click OK to finish.

200. – Add a 0.02" fillet to finish the part. Save as *'Cylindrical Cam'*.

Exercises: Build the following parts using the knowledge acquired in this lesson. Try to use the most efficient method to complete the model.

Eccentric Coupler

Notes:

- Both circles are centered horizontally (Right view.)
- Add a guide sketch at the bottom.
- Set the Start and End Conditions for the loft to "Normal to Profile."
- Make as Thin Feature *or* Shell it after making the loft feature.

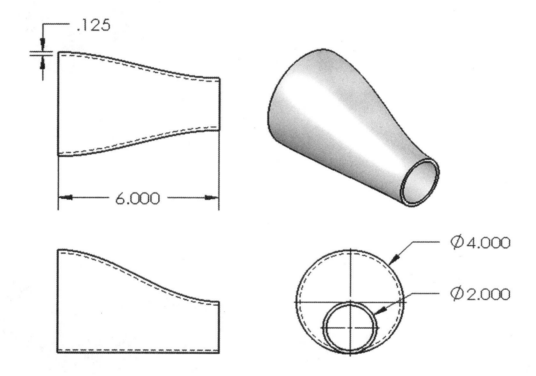

HINTS:

- Draw the 1" circle in the "*Right Plane.*"
- Make an Auxiliary Plane 6" parallel to the "*Right Plane.*"
- Draw a 2" circle in the Auxiliary Plane.
- Draw a sketch in the "*Front Plane*" to make the guide curve.
- Select the guide sketch in the "Guide Curves" selection box.

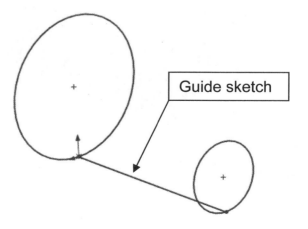

Guide sketch

Bent Coupler

Build the following part using a Loft feature and a shell. The part is 0.15″ thick.

Notes:
- Add a guide sketch along the right side of the part.
- Start and End Conditions "Normal to Profile."
- Make as Thin Feature or Shell after loft.

HINTS:
- Make Rectangular sketch first.
- Make Guide sketch.
- Make Auxiliary Plane perpendicular to Guide sketch at the end point.
- Make circular sketch in Auxiliary Plane.
- Make Loft using Guide sketch as a guide curve.
- Shell the part.

Guide sketch

Challenge Exercises: Build the *'Worm Gear'* and *'Offset Shaft'* complete gears using the knowledge learned so far with the information given. High resolution images at mechanicad.com.

DISCLOSURE: The gears modeled in this tutorial are not intended for manufacturing, nor is this tutorial meant to be a gear design guide. Its sole purpose is to show the reader how to apply the learned knowledge using a simplified version of the gears.

- **Offset Shaft**: Add the following sketch in the "*Front Plane*", Exit the sketch. Rename it "*Gear Width*." This is be the length of the full size helix.

- Build two reference planes parallel to the "*Right Plane*", one at each end of the "*Gear Width*" sketch.

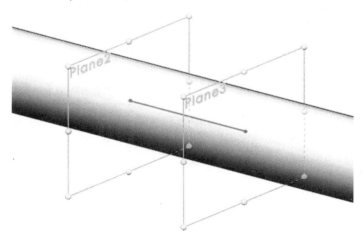

- Add the gear's profile sketch in the "*Front Plane*", at the left side of the "*Gear Width*" sketch. Exit the sketch and rename "*Thread Profile*."

- In the plane located at the left of the "*Gear Width*" sketch add a new sketch, use the "Convert Entities" drop down icon to select "**Intersection Curve**", this command will create sketch entities at the intersection of the selected surface(s) and the current sketch plane. This tool is particularly useful when we have irregular surfaces intersecting the sketch plane. In this case it works the same as "Convert Entities", but for oblique surfaces it's the best option to obtain the intersection of the surface and the sketch plane.

- Make the Helix 1" Height with a 0.25" Pitch

- Make the first sweep using the profile and the first helix.

- In the plane at the right of the "*Gear Width*" sketch add a sketch to start a second Helix using "Convert Entities", and make the helix activating the "Taper Helix" option with a 7deg taper.

H:	0in
P:	0.25in
Rev:	0
Dia:	0.575in

H:	0.625in
P:	0.25in
Rev:	2.5
Dia:	0.422in

Helix/Spiral2

Defined By:

Height and Pitch

Parameters

- Constant pitch
- Variable pitch

Height:

0.625in

Pitch:

0.250in

Reverse direction

Start angle:

90.00deg

- Clockwise
- Counterclockwise

Taper Helix

7.00deg

Taper outward

- Add a sketch at the flat end of the thread using "**Convert Entities**" to use as the profile for the tapered helix (Rear view), and make the sweep.

- Repeat a helix and sweep for the other side

- Add a 0.015" fillet to round the edges of the thread. Save as '*Offset Shaft Gear*' and close.

- **Worm Gear**: Create a parallel plane 0.95" above to the "*Top Plane*."

- Add the following sketch in the plane made in the previous step, exit the sketch and rename it "*Path*."

- Add a new auxiliary plane perpendicular to the "*Path*" sketch. Rename it "*Profile Plane*."

- Add this sketch in the "*Right Plane*" and make a revolved cut.

- In the "*Profile Plane*" add the following sketch. This will be the gear cut profile. Locate the sketch using the "Path" sketch at the indicated point. Exit the sketch and rename "*Gear Profile*"

- Make a "**Cut Sweep**" using the "*Path*" and "*Gear Profile*" sketches (We can also make a "Cut Extrude" in this case works the same.)

- Add a 0.015" fillet at the bottom of the sweep cut.

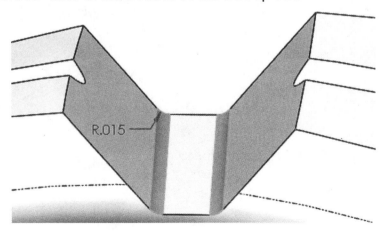

233

- Make 22 copies of the Cut-Sweep and the previous fillet. Add a 0.015" fillet to the "*Cut-Revolve1*" and "*Cut-Revolve3*" to finish the gear.

Save as '*Worm Gear Complete*' and close.

Engine Project Parts: Make the following components to build the engine. Save the parts using the name provided. High resolution images at mechanicad.com.

Hint: Make a revolved boss with the option "Thin Feature."

SKETCH FOR WRAP FEATURE
7 INSTANCES 0.5" APART

R.125

.115

1.850

.500

Ø.250

30°

6.000

.250

CIRCULAR PATTERN
WITH WRAP FEATURE
8 INSTANCES

Exhaust
DIMENSIONS: INCHES
MATERIAL: Chrome Stainless Steel

Ø1.250

Ø1.000

R.250

R.750

.750

4.750

.050

R1.000

Ø1.000

Ø1.750

Ø1.250

R.375

.050

SECTION A-A

4X Ø .266 THRU ALL

1.750

1.750

R.250

A

A

235

Final Parts for the Engine Project: The following components are the last required to complete the engine. Save the parts using the name provided.

A help sheet with a sequence of features is located in the Appendix for each of the last three parts. High resolution images at mechanicad.com.

Crank Case Top (2 Pages)

Crank Case Top
DIMENSIONS: INCHES
MATERIAL: Cast Alloy Steel   PAGE 2 OF 2

R.050

DETAIL D
SCALE 1 : 1

10°

E

1.250

1.500

THREAD
PITCH 0.075"
3.5 TURNS

FILLET THREAD
R.010

R.010

.030

∅.395

∅.275

.040

THREAD
PROFILE

DETAIL E
SCALE 4 : 1

SECTION B-B

.250

2.500

.250

.125
.250

R.125

R.500

.125

4.000

.375

Ø1.250

Ø1.500

3X Ø.107 ↧.432 ↧.276
6-32 UNC

3.000

60°

DETAIL A
SCALE 1 : 1

Ø2.000

Ø1.750

R.050

16X Ø.213 THRU
1/4-28 UNF THRU

Oil Pan
DIMENSIONS: INCHES
MATERIAL: Cast Alloy Steel

16X Ø.213 THRU
1/4-28 UNF THRU

5.500

8.000

.200

R.050

70°

2.000

A

B

B

6.500

16X Ø.213 THRU
1/4-28 UNF THRU

2.150

1.200

.750

.750

.325

Ø.450

Engine Block
DIMENSIONS: INCHES
MATERIAL: Cast Alloy Steel

Extra Credit: Visit our web site to download details for the *Gas Grill* project as well as the finished parts for this book, higher resolution images of the exercises and some extra topics not covered in the book. Build these components and after the Assembly lesson make the Gas Grill assembly.

http://mechanicad.com/download.html

Detail Drawing

Now that we have completed modeling the components, it's time to make the 2D detail drawings for manufacturing. In SolidWorks, first we make the 3D models and from them we can derive the 2D drawings. By deriving the drawing from the solid model, the 2D drawing is linked and associated to the part. This means that if the part is changed, the drawing will be updated and vice versa. Drawing files in SolidWorks have the extension *.slddrw and each drawing can contain multiple sheets, each corresponding to a different printed page of the same or different 3D models (either parts *or* assemblies.)

SolidWorks offers a simple to use environment where we can easily create 2D drawings of parts and assemblies. In this section we'll cover Part drawings only. Assembly drawings will be covered after the assembly section. We will add different model views, annotations, dimensions, sections and details necessary for manufacturing to fabricate the component without missing any details. In this section we will also introduce a new concept called **Configurations**, which allow us to show different versions of the same part, for example, a version for the part as it comes out of the foundry and a version for the machine shop with all the details for machining the finished part.

We can create our 2D drawings using any of the many dimensioning standards available in the industry. In this book we will use the ANSI standard. Once in a drawing, the dimensioning standard can be easily changed to a different one by going to the menu "**Tools, Options**" and selecting the "Document Properties" tab. In the Drafting Standard section we can select the desired detailing standard. It is important to note that after changing a standard, SolidWorks will change the dimension styles, arrow head type, etc. accordingly. For more information on changing units see the Appendix.

The detailing environment of SolidWorks is a true What-You-See-Is-What-You-Get interface. When we make a new drawing, we are asked what size of drawing sheet we want to use unless we are using a template with a predefined sheet size. This size corresponds to the printed sheet size. Do not be too concerned about selecting the right sheet size, as it can be changed to a larger or smaller size at any time if we find that our drawing will not fit the current sheet.

Notes:

Drawing One: The Housing

Notes:

In this lesson we'll learn how to make configurations of a part, how to make a multi sheet drawing with the different configurations, add views including sections and details, change a drawing's view display style, move the views within the drawing sheet, import model dimensions and manipulate them. The detail drawing of the *'Housing'* part will follow the next sequence.

Add Configuration	Make new drawing	Insert drawing views	Shaded Isometric
Add Section view	Add Detail view	Import Annotations	Arrange Annotations
Add drawing sheet	Change Configuration	Add new Detail view	Import Missing Annotations

201. - The first thing we need to do is to make a new **Configuration** of the *'Housing'* part. SolidWorks' Configurations allow us to make slightly or considerably different versions of a part without having to make a new part, in order to show or document different states of a component or a different but similar part. For our example, we'll have a configuration of the *'Housing'* as it comes out of the foundry, and another of the finished part for the machine shop. We can configure many different things including dimensions, tolerance, suppressed features, etc.

Open the *'Housing'* part and activate the **"ConfigurationManager"** tab. The Configuration Manager is where we can add, delete and change between the different configurations of a part. We can find it at the top of the FeatureManager; it's the third tab at the top as indicated.

There is always one configuration called *'Default'*. Once the ConfigurationManager is selected, we can add a new configuration by right-mouse-clicking at the top of the ConfigurationManager in the part's name, in this case *'Housing'*, and selecting the "**Add Configuration**…" option. Name the new configuration *"Forge"* and click OK. Adding a description is optional.

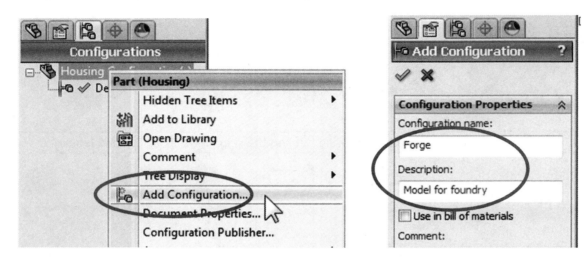

After adding the configuration you may be warned about the material's appearance, and if you'd like to link the display state to show the material's appearance in the configuration. Press "Yes" if asked.

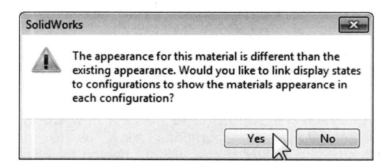

202. - After adding the new configuration, we'll rename the "Default" configuration. Right-mouse-click in it and select "Properties" to change its name to *"Machined."* As before, adding a description is optional. Click OK when finished.

Configurations can also be renamed using the slow double click method.

203. - In the ConfigurationManager, the yellow colored configuration with the Green checkmark is the currently active configuration; all others are grayed out. To switch to a different configuration we can double-click an inactive configuration's name or right-mouse-click and select "**Show Configuration**" from the pop-up menu.

204. - Activate the *"Forge"* configuration (it will have the green checkmark), and change to the FeatureManager tab. Notice that next to the name of the part at the top of the FeatureManager we can see the name of the currently active configuration.

In the *"Forge"* configuration, we'll "**Suppress**" all the features that cannot be made when casting the part, and make the holes smaller to machine them to size later. Essentially, suppressing a feature will tell SolidWorks to *NOT* make it. It will still be listed in the FeatureManager, but will be grayed out. For all practical purposes a suppressed feature doesn't exist in the model, and, since it is not created, the model's mass properties will be affected.

205. - First, select the *'1/4-20 Tapped Hole1'* from the FeatureManager (which cannot be made in a foundry), and from the pop-up toolbar select the "**Suppress**" icon. After suppressing a feature its name will be grayed out. Remember that **we are not deleting it**; it's still there, but it is suppressed.

Notice that the two features after the one we suppressed, *"CirPattern1"* and *"Mirror3"*, were also suppressed. This is because these features are 'children' of the *"1/4-20 Tapped Hole1."* Look at it this way: if there is no tapped hole, we cannot pattern it, and if there is no pattern, we cannot mirror it either. The "Parent/Child" relations are created when we add features that use or reference existing features in the model. For example, when a sketch is created in a face, the face becomes a parent to the sketch. If the face is deleted, so will the sketch and so on.

 Parent/Child relations can be found by right-mouse-clicking on a feature and from the pop-up menu selecting "**Parent/Child.**"

206. - Now suppress the *"#6-32 Tapped Hole1"* and the *"Slot"* features. All the children features of *"Slot"* are suppressed as well.

207. - The reverse process to Suppressing a feature is "**Unsuppress**." Select a suppressed feature and click on the "Unsuppress" icon (the icon with the arrow pointing up.) Do not Unsuppress any features at this time; we are just explaining how to do it, we'll get to it later.

Our "*Forge*" configuration now looks like this:

When Unsuppressing a feature with children in the FeatureManager, the child features need to be Unsuppressed individually. To Unsuppress a feature and all its children, use the menu "**Edit, Unsuppress with Dependents**." If a Child feature is unsuppressed, all of its parent features will be unsuppressed at the same time.

208. - Next we want to change the value of the two circular cuts for the *"Forge"* configuration. Make sure the *"Forge"* configuration is active. If the "**Instant 3D**" command is active, select a face of the first cut in the screen or double click in the feature in the FeatureManager, or in one of its faces in the graphics area to reveal the feature's dimensions. Right-mouse-click in the diameter dimension and select the "**Configure Dimension**" option from the pop-up menu.

In the "**Modify Configurations**" table, change the value of the diameter in the *"Forge"* configuration to 2.200″. The idea is to have a smaller hole made in the forge, and machine it to size later (*Machined* configuration.) Leave the "*Machined*" configuration value as 2.500″ and click "OK" to finish.

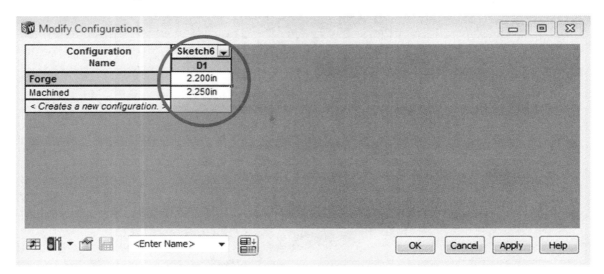

209. - A different way to configure dimensions is by double-clicking a dimension, and when the "Modify" dialog comes up we can select which configurations to modify; after adding configurations, the "Modify" dialog adds a configuration icon at the end of the value. This icon helps us define if we want to change the dimension's value for "This Configuration", "All Configurations" or "Specify Configurations." Keep in mind that this icon will only be visible *IF* we have more than one configuration in the part. Double-click the *"Shaft Hole"* feature to display it's dimensions, double-click the diameter dimension change the value to 0.55". Make sure we are only changing the value of this configuration by selecting the configuration button and selecting "This Configuration." Click OK to finish.

210. - An easy way to work with configurations is by viewing both the **FeatureManager** and the **ConfigurationManager** at the same time by splitting the FeatureManager pane. Move the mouse pointer to the top of the FeatureManager and look for the "split" feedback icon, then click-and-drag down. We can view Features in the top pane and Configurations in the bottom pane.

Now that we have made some changes to the *"Forge"* configuration, double click on each configuration to activate it and see what each one of them looks like. Notice the missing features (suppressed) and different sizes of the holes in the *"Forge"* configuration. Save these changes to the *'Housing'* part.

Forge   Machined

 We can add as many configurations as needed, but when we have more than 2 or 3 configurations it is easier to manage them with a table. Design Tables are very powerful and will be covered later in the book.

211. - Now, in order to make the detail drawing of the *'Housing'* part, make sure the *"Forge"* configuration is active, and then select the menu **"File, Make Drawing from Part"** or from the **"New"** document drop-down command. This way we'll make the first drawing using the *"Forge"* configuration. We'll make the *"Machined"* configuration drawing later.

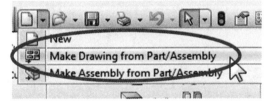

212. - We are now presented with the option to select a sheet size to use for this drawing. For Paper Size select "B-Landscape", and turn off the **"Display Sheet Format"** option.

The "Sheet Format" is the part of the drawing that contains the title block and related annotations. It will be covered in detail later. We are not including it now for easier visualization of this drawing.

213. - After selecting the sheet size, a new drawing is opened and SolidWorks is ready for us to choose the views that we want in the drawing. The "**View Palette**" is automatically displayed, make sure the "Auto-start projected view" option is active, as this option will save us time when locating the rest of the views.

214. - From the "**View Palette**" drag-and-drop the "Front" view onto the sheet.

215. - Locate the "Front" view in the lower left part of the sheet where we have enough room to add the other views. After locating the "Front" view on the sheet, SolidWorks automatically starts the "**Projected View**" command; to add the

rest of the views, move the mouse in the direction of the view needed, and click to locate it on the sheet. As a guide, after adding the "Front" view, move the mouse pointer above it and click to locate the "Top" view (you will be able to see a preview), then click above to the right where the Isometric view will be and finally click to the right to locate the "Right" view. When we are done adding views, click "OK" or press the "Esc" key to finish. Your drawing should now look approximately like this:

216. - Click to Select the "Front" view in the graphics area and change the Display Style to "**Hidden Lines Visible**" from the view's PropertyManager. This change will update the rest of the views, since they were projected from the "Front" view and by default they use the parent view's display style.

 The option to set the default display style and tangent edge visibility for new views can be changed in the menu "**Tools, Options, System Options**" under "**Display Style**."

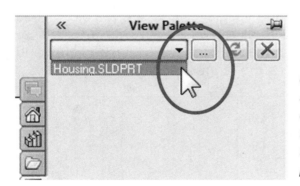

Adding standard and projected drawing views

*When we make a new drawing from a part using the menu "**Make Drawing from Part**", SolidWorks automatically displays the "**View Palette**." However, if we make a new drawing using the "**New Document**" icon, we get a different behavior. To test it, select the "**New Document**" icon and create a Drawing by selecting the "**Drawing**" template using the same settings as before. In this case, we are presented with an empty drawing. (If the "Model View" command is loaded, cancel it.)*

To activate the View Palette, click in the View Palette icon from the Task Pane on the right side of the screen to display it.

View Palette
Click to display this task pane tab.

Once the "View Palette" is displayed, we can browse for a part or assembly or select one of the open documents from the drop-down list. At this time we'll be able to drag and drop the views onto the sheet as we did in the previous step.

217. - Now that we have the views in place, we want to show the Isometric view in "**Shaded with Edges**" mode. Click to select the "Isometric" view on the screen, and click the "**Shaded with Edges**" icon either in the "**Display Style**" toolbar or in the PropertyManager as in the previous step. Notice the dotted line around the view; this is an indication that the view is selected. Using this procedure, we can change any drawing view to any display mode as needed.

218. - In the drawing views we may or may not want to see the tangent edges. A tangent edge is where a curved face and a flat face have a tangent transition, as in fillets. SolidWorks has three different ways to show them: Visible, With Font, or Removed. Right-mouse-click inside the Front view, and from the pop-up menu select the option "**Tangent Edge, Tangent Edges Removed**." Repeat for the Top and Right views.

 The differences between tangent edge display types are visible in this table. "**Tangent Edges Visible**" shows all model edges with a solid line, "**Tangent Edges with Font**" shows tangent edges with a dashed line, and "**Tangent Edges Removed**" eliminates the tangent edges from the view.

| Tangent Edges Visible | Tangent Edges With Font | Tangent Edges Removed |

 The default Tangent Edge display settings can also be changed in the menu "**Tools, Options, System Options, Drawings, Display Style**." For the rest of this book we'll use "Tangent Edges With Font."

219. - The next thing we want to do in the drawing is to move the views to arrange them in the sheet. To move a view, click-and-drag the view either from the View border or any model edge in the view.

220. - Click-and-drag the drawing views in the drawing sheet and arrange them as shown, with "**Tangent Edges Removed**" for all views, and the Isometric with "**Shaded with Edges**" display. This layout will allow enough space to import the dimensions into the drawing. Make sure the drawing's units are set to inches and three decimal places.

 Notice the toolbars available in the CommandManager were automatically changed to match the detail drawing environment in which we are now. The Features tab was replaced by View Layout and Annotation, with tools and commands for detailing.

221. - To make an easier to read drawing we'll add a section of the Right view. Select the "**Section View**" command from the View Layout tab in the CommandManager.

222. - From the "**Section View**" properties, select "Vertical" from the "Cutting Line" options; in the graphics area move close to the center of the "Right" view the section line preview is displayed automatically. To locate the section line click when it snaps to the center. After selecting the center select the green checkmark from the pop-up toolbar to make a simple section.

 We can zoom in or out in the Drawing using the mouse scroll wheel. SolidWorks will zoom in or out at the location of the mouse pointer.

223. - Now, move the cursor above the view, and using the center of the edge as a reference, draw a line starting *above* the view and all the way across through the Right view as shown.

224. - Immediately after selecting OK, move the mouse and you'll see a dynamic preview showing the section of the *'Housing'*; the last thing to do is to add the section view in the sheet. Move the mouse to the left and click between the Front and Right views to locate it. If needed, after locating the Section view move the other views to arrange and space them.

Using the mouse wheel we can manipulate the drawing view. Use the wheel to zoom in and out, and the middle mouse button (Press the wheel down) to move the drawing (Pan). We can do this while positioning the section view or any other view.

Selecting the Section View we can see its Properties, where we can change different options such as the Section Label, reverse the section direction ("Flip Direction"), Display Style, Scale, etc. Change the Section View's display style to "**Hidden Lines Removed**" for clarity if needed. By default, the section will inherit the display style of the view from which it was made.

SECTION A-A

225. - The next step is to add a "**Detail View.**" Detail views allow us to zoom in an area of the drawing. From the View Layout tab in the CommandManager, select the "**Detail View**" icon. After selecting it we are asked to draw a circle in the area that we want to make a detail of..

 To draw sketch elements without automatically adding geometric relations to other elements, hold down the "Ctrl" key while drawing. This technique works in the part, assembly and detailing environments.

226. - Draw a circle in the upper left area of the "Section" view (try not to add automatic relations when drawing the circle), and just like the "Section" view…

SECTION A-A

…move the mouse to locate the Detail above the section using the dynamic preview. By default, detail views are two times bigger than the view they came from. This option can be changed in the menu "**Tools, Options, System Options, Drawings**" and change the "**Detail view scaling**" factor to multiply the scale of the view the detail came from.

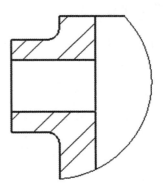

DETAIL B
SCALE 1 : 1

 If the detail is not as big as needed, click-and-drag the detail's circle and/or its center to resize and move the detail area; the Detail view will update dynamically, that is the reason why we don't want to add any geometric relations when drawing the detail's circle.

 Alternatively we can draw the circle (or any closed contour like ellipse, polygon or spline) and then select the "**Detail View**" icon.

227. - Now that we have all the views that we need in the drawing, the next step is to import the *'Housing's'* dimensions from the part into the drawing. If you remember, we added all the necessary dimensions to the part when it was modeled, and now we can import those dimensions into the detail drawing, effectively reducing the amount of work needed to complete this task.

Select "**Model Items**" from the Annotation tab in the CommandManager or go to the menu "**Insert, Model Items**."

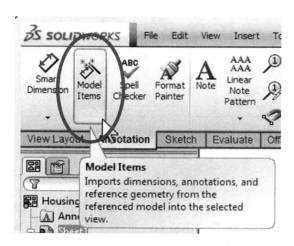

228. - In the "Model Items" options select the type of dimensions and annotations we want to import to the drawing. For this exercise select the options listed below. Remember to select "Source: Entire Model" to import the dimensions of the entire *'Housing'* , and activate the checkbox "**Import items into all views**" to add all dimensions to all views. "Dimensions Marked for Drawing" is selected by default, optionally we can activate "Hole Wizard Locations" to import the location of holes made with the Hole Wizard, "Hole Callout" to add the machining annotations to the holes made with the Hole Wizard, and Tolerenced Dimensions to import dimensions with tolerances.

Dimensions marked for drawing

Hole Wizard Locations

Tolerenced Dimensions

Hole callout

229. - After selecting OK, SolidWorks imports the dimensions and annotations to all views, arranging them automatically. Dimensions are first added to Detail views, then to Section views, and finally main views. The reason is because Detail Views show more model details, Section Views often show otherwise hidden features, and finally the main views show the major features. While SolidWorks makes a good job at adding dimensions to views, they are not always added to the view that best displays it, and here is where we have to do some work.

 If the drawing's dimensions are not the desired units and decimal places, change them in the menu "**Tools, Options, Document Properties, Units**" or from the Unit System button in the status bar.

230. - All the dimensions that were added to the part when we made it, including sketch and feature dimensions have been imported to the drawing. Now we need to arrange them in order to make the drawing easier to read. To arrange annotations in the drawing click-and-drag them as needed.

To move a dimension from one view to another, <u>hold down the "**Shift**" key, and while holding it down, drag the dimension</u> to the view where we want it. Remember that the dimension has to be dragged inside the border of the view wanted. Arrange the annotations as needed to make the drawing easy to read.

 Some of the dimensions added to a drawing view are incorrectly assigned and we need to move them to a different view. One way to tell which dimensions belong to a view is to move the view. All of the annotations attached will move.

231. - If missing, add the circle center marks using the "**Center Mark**" icon from the Annotation toolbar. Select "**Center Mark**" from the Annotation tab, and click on the circular edges to add center marks as needed. Click OK to finish. "**Centerlines**" can be added the same way by clicking on the cylindrical faces.

232. - Another thing that you may want to do is to reverse the arrows of a dimension. To do this, select the dimension and click on the dots in the arrow heads to reverse them. To delete a dimension that is duplicated or you don't want, select it and hit the "Delete" key. You only deleting it from the drawing and not from the part. If the dimensions are re-import to the drawing, SolidWorks will only bring back the missing dimensions. We'll cover more drawing views and annotations in the following drawings.

Extension lines from the dimensions can be dragged by their endpoints to change their location.

233. - Notice the tolerance for the *"Shaft Hole"* was carried over to the drawing from the part model. Be aware that if we need to add a tolerance or change a dimension's precision we can do it also in the detail drawing by selecting the dimension and changing the parameters in the PropertyManager *or* in the **"Dimension Palette"** after selecting a dimension. In this area we can change precision, tolerances, add notes, parentheses, etc.

Your finished drawing for the *"Forge"* configuration should now look like the next image.

DETAIL B
SCALE 1 : 1

SECTION A-A

234. - Now that the first sheet is finished, we have to add a second sheet to this drawing for the Machined configuration to get the machining details to complete the *'Housing's* detail drawing. We can add a second sheet and add views and dimensions just as we did for the first sheet, but a quicker way is to copy the drawing sheet we just finished and paste it, then modify it to add the missing details. In the FeatureManager, right-mouse-click in *"Sheet1"* and select "**Copy**", then repeat and select "**Paste**" *or* select the menu "**Edit, Paste**" (shortcut Ctrl+V.)

In the "**Insert Paste**" dialog box select the "After selected sheet" option. When asked about renaming the drawing views, click 'Yes'; this option will rename the section and detail views to use the next available view label, in our case **C** and **D**.

235. - Now we have a second sheet in the same drawing exactly the same as the first one, except for the view labels

 Drawing sheets can be renamed by right-mouse-clicking the sheet's tab or in the FeatureManager and selecting "Properties" or "Rename."

Rename *"Sheet1"* to *"Forge"* and *"Sheet1(2)"* to *"Machined."*

236. - Now we need to tell SolidWorks to show the *"Machined"* configuration in the second sheet. Select the "Machined" sheet's tab on the lower left corner of the screen to activate it. Since we made a copy of the *"Forge"* drawing, we need to change the configuration displayed to *"Machined."* Select the Front view in the screen; in the drawing's properties select the "Reference Configuration" drop-down menu and change to *"Machined."* Notice that the view is automatically updated in the graphics area. Repeat for the rest of the drawing views. The Section and Detail views will be updated after their parent views are updated.

237. - Once we have changed all the views to the *"Machined"* configuration, we can repeat the "**Model Items**" command to import the missing dimensions and annotations in this configuration. Be sure to include the "Hole Wizard Locations" and "Hole Callout" buttons. Arrange the newly imported dimensions and annotations as needed. Note the holes made with the Hole Wizard includes annotations with machining information. After the missing dimensions are added arrange them as needed in the different drawing views.

238. - Add the missing center marks to the circular array of tapped holes. Select the "**Center Mark**" icon from the Annotation tab, click in one hole's edge, and then click in the Propagate icon to add Center Marks to all the holes in the array at the same time.

239. - To make the slot dimensions easier to view, we'll add a new detail view in the slot area. Add the missing dimensions using the "**Smart Dimension**" tool or move the imported dimensions from the Top view to the new detail view using the "Shift-Drag" method. Remember to add the missing "**Center marks** as well. Add any missing dimensions to complete the drawing.

DETAIL E
SCALE 1 : 1

4X ⌀ .107 ↧ .432
6-32 UNC ↧ .276

240. - Manually added dimensions and some notes are grey instead of black, because they are reference dimensions and not parametric, the difference is that a parametric dimension can be changed by double clicking in the drawing and the changes will be reflected in the part (and vice versa), and a reference dimension cannot be changed. In order to change the color of the reference annotations we can add a "Layer" (black color) and then assign the annotations to this layer.

If not visible, turn on the "Layer" toolbar. Go to the menu "**View, Toolbars, Layer**" or right-mouse-click in any toolbar and select "Layer." By default it is located in the lower left corner.

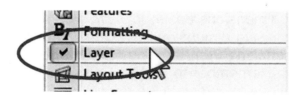

241. - Select the "Layer Properties" icon, here we can add, delete and modify layers as needed.

242. - In the "Layers" dialog select the "New" button to create a new layer. After it is created change its name to "Reference." The default color for new layers is black, so we don't need to change it. We'll add the reference annotations to this layer to display them using the layer color. Click OK to finish.

243. - To change an annotation (or model) to a different layer select it in the graphics area, and pick the new layer from the Layer toolbar. Select all reference annotations and then pick the "Reference" layer. Notice the color change.

244. - Rearrange the views as needed to make room for dimensions and annotations. Delete any duplicate dimensions to make drawing easier to read. Save the finished drawing as *'Housing'* and close the file. Note the file extension for drawings is *.slddrw.

Forge configuration finished drawing sheet.

Machined configuration finished drawing sheet.

Exercises: Make the detail drawings of the following Engine Project parts that were done in the Part Modeling section to match the drawing previously supplied to make each part. High resolution images at mechanicad.com.

Connecting Rod Bottom

Cylinder Gasket

Head Gasket

Shaft Seal Cover

Shaft Seal Gasket

Notes:

Drawing Two: The Side Cover

Ø3.250

Ø3.250

(Ø1.000)

Ø.625

Ø.250

Ø2.750

A

A

.125

.750

R.125

SECTION A-A

Notes:

In this lesson we'll review material previously covered, including how to add standard views, sections and importing annotations from the model to the drawing. We'll also learn how to add dimensions that are not present or in the desired format, change the sheet's scale and a view's scale.

The drawing of the *'Side Cover'* part will follow the next sequence.

Make new drawing	Insert drawing views	Section View	Import dimensions

Delete and arrange dimensions	Add Diameter Dimensions	Change Drawing and view scale

245. - We will repeat the process that we used with the *'Housing'* part Including adding a configuration to reinforce the material just covered. Open the *'Side Cover'* part and go to the Configuration Manager tab. Right-mouse-click in the part's name and select "Add Configuration." Enter the name "*Forge*" and click OK to continue.

246. - Rename the "*Default*" configuration to "*Machined*" using the slow-double-click method or the configuration properties.

247. - Split the FeatureManager with features at the top and configurations at the bottom. With the "*Forge*" configuration active suppress the hole feature, notice that the circular pattern is also suppressed because it's a child feature.

248. - Double click in the center hole to reveal the diameter dimension, and then double-click in it to change the diameter to 0.6" using the "This Configuration" button.

249. - With the "*Forge*" configuration active, select the menu "**File, Make Drawing from Par**t" or the icon from the "**New Document**" drop down menu to start the drawing.

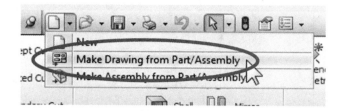

250. - For the *'Side Cover'* part we'll use the "A-Landscape" drawing template without sheet format. After selecting the sheet size add the Front, Top and Isometric views. Drag the Front view from the View Palette and project the Top and Isometric views from it.

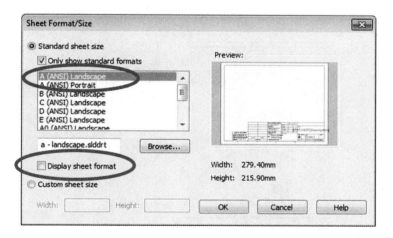

251. - From the "**View Palette**" drag and drop the Front view, and project the Top and Isometric views from it. Click OK when finished. Select the Front view, and if needed, change the Display Style to "**Hidden Lines Visible**" as we did in the previous exercise by selecting the view and changing it in the PropertyManager on the left.

For the Front and Top views change to "**Tangent Edges Removed**", and for the Isometric, choose "**Hidden Lines**" and "**Tangent Edges Visible**."

252. - Before adding the dimensions we need to add the centerline to the Top view. Select the "**Centerline**" command from the Annotations tab and click in the cylindrical surface of the Top view to add the centerline. Click OK to finish.

253. - To import the dimensions from the 3D model select **"Model Items"** from the Annotation tab or go to the menu **"Insert, Model Items."** For "Source/Destination" select "Entire Model" and activate the checkbox "Import items into all views" and click OK to add the dimensions.

254. - Delete and arrange the dimensions as shown. We'll add the diameter dimensions in the next step.

255. - Select the "**Smart Dimension**" tool and manually add the missing diameter dimensions.

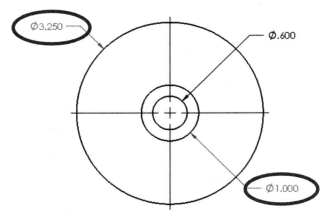

256. - Add a new (black) layer using the "**Layer**" command and change the added diameter dimensions to it to show them in black. Arrange the views as shown to finish the "*Forge*" configuration.

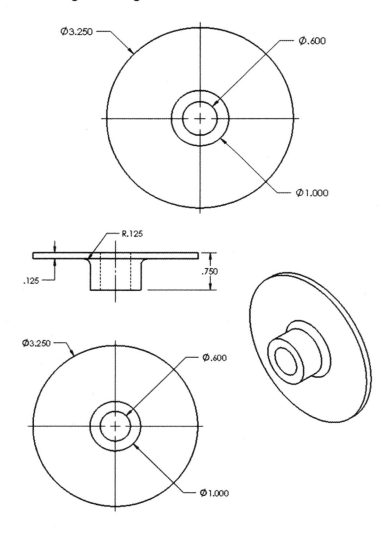

257. - Now we need to add a second sheet to our drawing to add the "*Machined*" configuration drawing. Instead of copying and pasting a complete sheet as we did with the '*Housing*', we'll only copy the Front view. Select the "**Add Sheet**" icon at the lower left corner and rename the sheets to show "*Forge*" and "*Machined*" respectively.

258. - Select the "*Forge*" sheet, click to select the Front view and either press **Ctrl-C** or the menu "**Edit, Copy**" to copy the view. Select the "*Machined*" view and press **Ctrl-V** or the menu "**Edit, Paste**" to paste the view. Select it and from the view's properties select the "Machined" configuration from the "Reference Configuration" drop down list.

259. - To add the Top and Isometric views go to the View Layout tab, select the Front view and click in the "Projected View" icon.

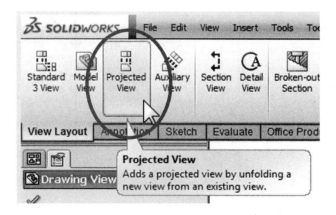

260. - Move the mouse above to add the Top view, move to the top right and add the Isometric view. Click OK to finish. Change the Isometric view to "Hidden Lines Removed" and "Tangent Edge Visible."

261. - Add a vertical section using the **"Section View"** icon from the View Layout. Select the "Vertical" option, click to locate the section line in the center of the Front view, click OK and locate the section view to the right.

SECTION A-A

262. - Use the "**Center Mark**" tool to add the center marks in the Front view. Select one of the holes, and then click in the "Propagate" icon to add all the holes at the same time. Click OK to finish.

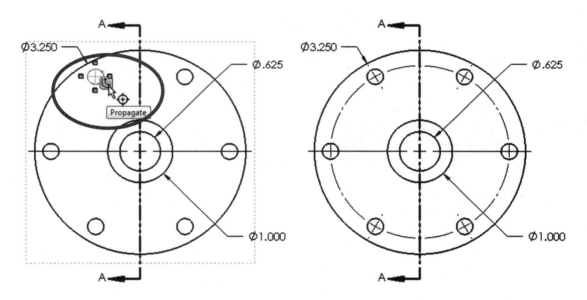

263. - Select "**Model Items**" from the Annotation tab to import the missing dimensions to the "*Machined*" configuration drawing. Use the "Entire Model" and "Import items into all views" options. Under Dimensions select "Hole Wizard Locations", "Hole Callout" and "Tolerenced Dimensions." Click OK to finish.

SECTION A-A

264. - Before we add the missing diameter dimensions select the new layer created early in the "Layer" toolbar. It will be called "Layer0" unless it was renamed. We have two additional layers, one is to define annotations per drafting standard and the other to None.

265. - Using the "**Smart Dimension**" tool add the missing diameter dimensions as shown in the next image. Note that with the new layer selected the new dimensions are added to it and are shown in black.

262. - When adding the hole's circle dimension we can see that the dimension added is displayed as a radial dimension. Right-mouse-click in it and from the pop-up menu select "Display Options, Show as Diameter."

263. - Dimensions manually added to a drawing can be displayed with a parenthesis to indicate it as a **Reference Dimension.** Reference dimensions are used to provide additional information to the drawing and don't have a tolerance. They should *NOT* to be used for manufacturing or inspection. For this drawing the 1" diameter is not a critical dimension, so we'll mark it as a reference. To add a parenthesis, select the dimension and from the Property Manager click in the "Parenthesis" icon.

 The option to add parentheses by default to reference dimensions is set in the menu "**Tools, Options, Document Properties, Dimensions, Add parentheses by default**." This is an option set by document and is not a system option.

264. - Another way to add or remove parentheses, as well as other options, is to use the "**Dimension Palette**." When we select one or more dimensions the dimension palette appears near the dimension; move the mouse over it to expand the "**Dimension Palette**" window. Here we can change a dimension's parameters including parenthesis, tolerance, precision, etc.

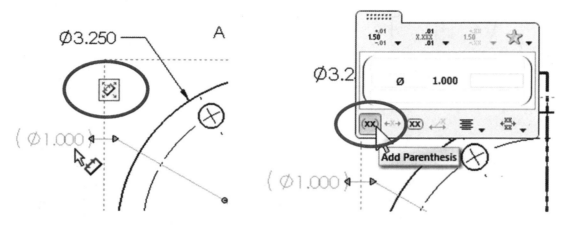

265. - In some instances the drawing sheet is too big or too small for the views. We can change the sheet's scale to make the views fit better. In this case, we need to change the sheet's scale to be 1:1. Make a right-mouse-click *in the sheet* (not a drawing view), or in the FeatureManager in the sheet's name, from the pop-up menu select "Properties."

 In pop-up menus notice the commands are grouped under a heading; in this case the options for "*Sheet (Machined)*" are listed.

288

266. - From the options box, make sure we are using a scale of 1:1, "Third angle" projection to match the book images and click OK to finish.

The "Type of projection" refers to how the views are projected from the 3D model. The "**First angle**" projection is widely used in Europe and the "**Third angle**" projection is more commonly used in America. This is a document property saved in the template. See the Appendix for more information in creating and using templates.

267. - After arranging the views and dimensions, we notice that the Isometric view is too big to fit in our sheet, so we'll change the view's scale.

Select the Isometric view in the graphics area, and from its PropertyManager, change the view scale to 1:2 from the "**Use custom scale**" drop down menu in the "Scale" options box.

268. - Our drawing is finished; save using the part's name and close the file.

SECTION A-A

Exercises: Make the detail drawings of the following Engine Project parts that were done in the Part Modeling section to match the drawing previously supplied to make each part.

Intake

Oil Pan Gasket

Sealed Needle Bearing

Add three configurations to show the different steps to model the part and match the original drawing suppressing features as needed.

Notes:

Drawing Three: The Top Cover

SECTION A-A

DETAIL B
SCALE 1 : 1

All rounds 0.032" *unless* otherwise specified
Material: Cast Alloy Steel
Volume: 1.82 cu-in
Weight: 0.48 Lb
Designer: Alejandro Reyes

Notes:

269. - In this lesson we'll review previously covered material, the section view option "Display only surface", adding Notes, Ordinate dimensions, and adding custom file properties to part and assembly files for use in drawings and bills of materials. The drawing of the *'Top Cover'* will follow the next sequence.

Make new drawing	Insert drawing views	Section View	Detail View

Import/Add Dimensions	Add Ordinate Dimensions	Add notes

270. - Open the *'Top Cover'* part and select the **"Make Drawing from Part /Assembly"** icon as we've done before. Select the drawing template with an "A-Landscape" sheet size without sheet format.

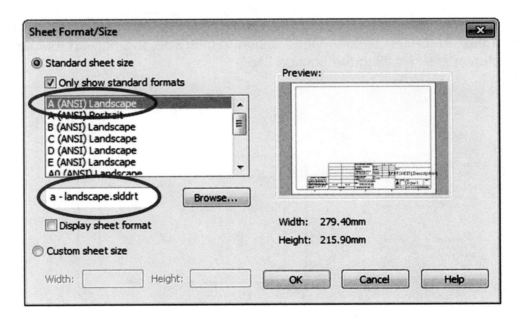

271. - Click-and-drag the Front view from the "**View Palette**" onto the sheet, and add Top, Bottom, Right and Isometric views. Change the display style to "Hidden Lines" and "Tangent Edges Removed" for all views except the Isometric, which we'll change to "Tangent Edges Visible."

272. - The next step is to make a section through the Top view to get more information about the cross section of the cover. Select the "**Section View**" icon from the View Layout tab, click in the "Horizontal" section icon and place the section line *approximately* through the middle of the Top view as indicated. Click OK in the pop-up toolbar and locate the new section view just below it.

 If the "Auto-start section view" option is checked, the pop-up toolbar is not shown after locating the section line.

273. - After locating the section view, you may have to activate the "Flip Direction" button to reverse the direction of the section view. Also check the **"Display only cut face(s)"** option to show only the section's surface ignoring the rest of the model behind the section line, the effect of activating this option is as if we had only taken a thin slice of the part at the section line.

 The direction of the section view can also be reversed by a double click in the section line. If the section is reversed this way, the drawing may have to be rebuilt.

274. - To get an even better view of the cross section, we'll make a detail of the right side of "Section A-A." Select the **"Detail View"** icon and draw a circle as shown; locate the detail below the Right view and distribute the views evenly in the sheet. If Center marks are automatically added, delete them for clarity.

SECTION A-A

275. - When we make detail and section views and make a mistake, or we are simply not happy with the result and delete the view, SolidWorks increases the *new view label* in the sheet's properties to the next available letter, unless the option is set in the menu "**Tools, Options, System Options, Drawings, Reuse view letters from deleted auxiliary, detail, and section views**." Any section, detail or auxiliary view's label can be changed at any time by selecting the view and changing the view's letter in its properties.

DETAIL B
SCALE 1 : 1

276. - The next step is to import the model dimensions from the part. Go to the menu "**Insert, Model Items**", remember to select "Import items into all views" and "Entire Model."

277. - Delete and arrange the dimensions as needed to match the next image.

278. - Add a dimension to the edge indicated in the bottom view. When adding a dimension to an arc, SolidWorks automatically defaults to a radial dimension. When selecting a circle we get the diameter dimension.

279. - In this example we want to show the dimension as a diameter, not a radius. To change it right-mouse-click in the dimension, and from the pop-up toolbar select "**Display options, Display as Diameter**."

 To change the dimension to radial again repeat the previous step and select "**Display as Radius**."

280. - In certain circumstances its convenient to add "**Ordinate Dimensions**" to a drawing. Ordinate dimensions have to be added manually unless they were added to a sketch and are being imported. Click anywhere in the graphics area with the right mouse button, and from the pop-up menu select "**More Dimensions, Vertical Ordinate**" or from the "Smart Dimension" icon's drop down menu.

281. - To add ordinate dimensions click first to select the edge that will be the zero reference, then click to locate the "0" dimension and finally click on each horizontal line or vertex to add a dimension to it. The Ordinate Dimensions will be automatically aligned and jogged if needed. In the Detail view, select the lower edge to be the zero reference, click to the right to locate it, and click in the rest of the edges to add the dimensions.

 If after adding the ordinate dimensions a dimension is missed, right mouse click in any of the ordinate dimensions, select "**Add to Ordinate**" and click in the edge/vertex that was missed to dimension it.

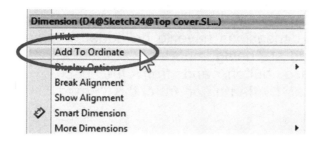

282. - Now we are going to add a note to the drawing. Notes are common in drawings to communicate important information, such as material, finish, dates, designer, etc. To add a note to our drawing, select the "**Note**" icon from the Annotation tab or the menu "**Insert, Annotations, Note**"...

...and click in the drawing to locate the note; the **Formatting toolbar** is automatically displayed next to the note (unless it's already visible as a toolbar.) This toolbar is similar to many Windows' applications to change font and style.

283. - After the note is located in the drawing, we can type and format it just as we would in a word processor. If multiple notes are needed, instead of OK, click in the drawing to locate the next note and repeat the process. Feel free to experiment with different fonts and styles. Click OK in the PropertyManager when finished adding the note. To edit an existing note double-click on it.

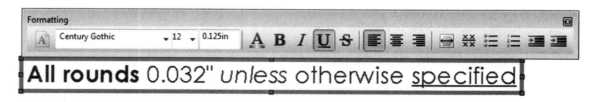

284. - Parts and assemblies can be given specific "**Document Properties**" that contain user defined data (a designer's name, department, part number, etc.) or parametric information that updates if the model changes, like a component's material, weight, volume, surface area, etc.

Open the '*Top Cover*' part file (*Top Cover.sldprt*), and select the menu "**File, Properties**." In the "Summary Information" window select the "Custom" tab. This is the area where Custom Properties are defined for a document. For this example we'll add three properties that are linked to the part's Volume, Weight and Material, and a user defined property with the designer's name.

 To open a part file directly from the drawing, click in the part in a drawing view and select the "**Open Part**" command from the pop-up menu.

285. - In the "Property Name" column, click in the first cell and select "Material" from the drop down menu; in the "Type" column "Text" is automatically selected; click in the "Value/Text Expression" cell, and from the drop down menu select "Material." SolidWorks fills in the correct expression to make the property's value equal to "Cast Alloy Steel", which is the material we had assigned to this part.

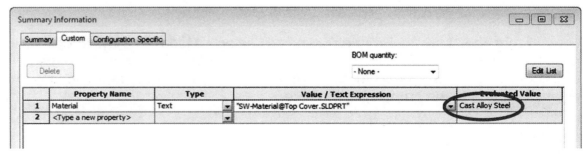

After adding a property a new empty row appears. In the second property name enter "*Volume*" and select "Volume" from the value drop-down menu, for the third property name select "Weight" and "Mass" for the value, and for the last property type "*MyName*" in the "Property Name" and fill in your name for the value. Click OK when done and save your changes to the *'Top Cover'* part file.

 Property names not listed can be typed in, or if they will be also used in other documents, select "Edit List" to add them to the drop down list of properties used for all components.

286. - Using the menu "Window" go back to the *'Top Cover – Sheet1'* drawing. Add a note as we just did and type: "*Material:*" While still editing the note click in the "**Link to Property**" icon from the note's "Text Format" options.

From the "Link to Property" window, select "Model in view specified in sheet properties"; this will tell the note to use the Custom Properties from the part in the drawing. Then select "Material" from the drop down list and click on OK when done to add the property to the note.

Depending on how SolidWorks is configured, you may see in the note "*$PRPSHEET: Material*", this is the code used by SolidWorks to read part properties. If you see this code it will be replaced by the component's property value after we finish the note. Your note should now look like this:

287. -The rest of the parametric notes can be added the same way. Press "Enter" to add a new row in the note; type "*Volume:*", add the link to the "Volume" property; in the next row in the note type "*Weight:*" and add the link to the "Weight" property; finally type "*Designer:*" and link to the "MyName" property.

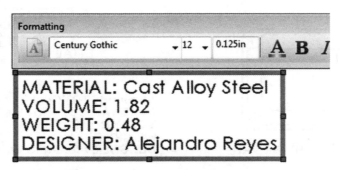

One drawback of using parametric notes that return a numeric value is that the units of measure are not listed, and they have to be either manually added to the note or by adding a custom property to the part/assembly with the units. The values are always displayed using the units used in the part. In our example the volume is measured in cubic inches and the weight is in pounds. We can manually add the units to the note. After formatting, the final note will look like this:

305

All rounds 0.032" *unless* otherwise specified
MATERIAL: Cast Alloy Steel
VOLUME: 1.82 cu-in
WEIGHT: 0.48 lb
DESIGNER: Alejandro Reyes

If any of these properties changes in the part, the note in the drawing will be updated. For example, if the model changes size, the volume and mass values will be updated accordingly.

288. - Add a new layer (black) and move the reference dimensions to it. Save the drawing and close the file.

SECTION A-A
4.000

R.031

.500
.375
.250
.125
0

DETAIL B
SCALE 1 : 1

Ø.500

4X Ø .150 THRU ALL

2.625

.375

R.250

All rounds 0.032" *unless* otherwise specified
MATERIAL: Cast Alloy Steel
VOLUME: 1.82 cu-in
WEIGHT: 0.48 lb
DESIGNER: Alejandro Reyes

Exercises: Make the detail drawing of the following Engine Project part that were done in the Part Modeling section to match the drawing previously supplied to make each part. High resolution images at mechanicad.com.

Cylinder Head

Notes:

Drawing Four: The Offset Shaft

.063 ← → ← .500 →

DETAIL A
SCALE 2 : 1

.500 ← 5.000 →
.063
.063

A

6.500

$\varnothing .600^{+.000}_{-.005}$

Material: Chrome Stainless Steel
Volume: 1.80 cu-in
Weight: 0.51 lb
Designer: Alejandro Reyes

Description: Part No. ABC-1234

Notes:

The *'Offset Shaft'* drawing, although a simple drawing, will help us reinforce previously covered commands including standard and detail views, importing dimensions, manipulating and modifying a dimension's appearance, notes and custom file properties, and we'll learn how to add a break to a view. In this exercise we will make Front, Right, detail and broken views, import model dimensions, add notes and modify their appearance following the next sequence:

Make new drawing	Insert drawing views	Detail View	Broken View

Import Dimensions	Arrange Dimensions	Add custom properties and notes

289. - Since we have already done a few drawings, we'll ask you to make a new drawing using the "A-Landscape" sheet size. Add the Front view by dragging it from the View Palette, and project the Right view. Change the display mode to "Hidden Lines Removed" as shown. Right mouse click in the sheet, select "Properties" and change the sheet's scale to 1:1. Add a detail view of the right side of the shaft as shown.

DETAIL A
SCALE 2 : 1

290. - For long slender elements like shafts, it's common practice to add a **Break** to shorten the view and save space in the drawing. To add a break in the front view, select the "**Break**" icon from the View Layout tab in the CommandManager or the menu "**Insert, Drawing View, Break**."

We are then presented with the "**Broken View**" dialog. If the Front view is not selected, click on it to tell SolidWorks which view to break. The Vertical Break option is selected by default, and all we have to do is select where the breaks will be in the view. Click near the right side to locate the first break line, and a second click near the left side to add the second break. Click OK to finish the command.

 If you need to modify the break lines' location, just click-and-drag them with the mouse. To delete a broken view, select a break line and delete it.

291. - You probably know what we are going to do now… Yes, import the dimensions from the part. Go to the menu "**Insert, Model Items**"; remember to select the "Import items into all views" and "Entire Model" options. In this case, SolidWorks added the dimensions almost as we need them, we'll just arrange them a little in the next step.

292. - Move the dimensions as shown in the next image; remember to hold down the "Shift" key while moving dimensions from one view to another.

293. - Open the *'Offset Shaft'* part file, and from the menu "**File, Properties**" add the same custom properties as we did in the *'Top Cover'*. Add a new property called "Description" and fill in a description of the shaft. For this example any description will do. We'll use this description in the drawing and the bill of materials later. The "Summary Information" window should look like this:

 If the values for volume and weight show as zeroes, you may have to close the file properties and rebuild the model. When you re-open the file properties window those values will be populated.

294. - Save the *'Offset Shaft'* part and go back to the drawing; add the notes using the "**Note**" tool from the Annotation tab. The user will have to type "*Material:*" "*Volume:*" "*Weight:*", "*Designer*" and "*Description*", and link to the corresponding property after each one. Remember to add the units of measure.

The finished note will be:

Material: Chrome Stainless Steel
Volume: 1.80 cu-in
Weight: 0.51 lb
Designer: Alejandro Reyes

Description: Part No. ABC-1234

295. - Save and close the drawing file.

DETAIL A
SCALE 2 : 1

Material: Chrome Stainless Steel
Volume: 1.80 cu-in
Weight: 0.51 lb
Designer: Alejandro Reyes

Description: Part No. ABC-1234

Notes:

Drawing Five: The Worm Gear

Notes:

In this lesson we'll review previously covered material and a couple of new options, like adding angular dimensions, changing a dimension's precision and adding chamfer dimensions as well as a Crop View and modifying the Sheet Format. The detail drawing of the *'Worm Gear'* will follow the next sequence.

Add Custom Properties	Make new drawing	Insert drawing views	Add view and Crop
Import and arrange Dimensions	Add Angular Dimension	Add chamfer Dimension	Modify Sheet format

296. - As we did in the previous drawing, we will first open the *'Worm Gear'* part and make a drawing, but before we do the drawing, we'll add custom properties to the part. With the *'Worm Gear'* part file open, select the menu **"File, Properties"** and complete it as shown next.

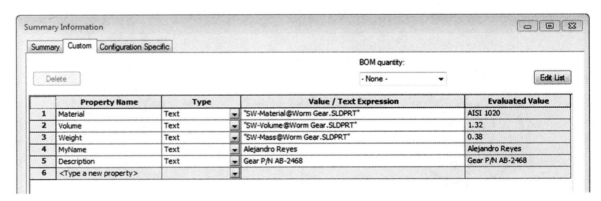

Select the **"Make Drawing from Part/Assembly"** icon. For the *'Worm Gear'* use the Drawing Template with an "A-Landscape" sheet size and leave the "Display Sheet Format" option active in the "Sheet Format/Size" window. We'll learn how to edit the sheet format in this exercise.

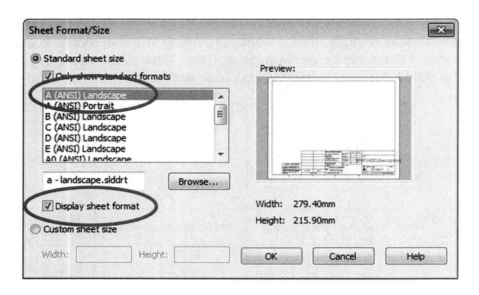

297. - Just as we've done in previous drawings, the first step is to add the main views for the model. Add the Front view from the "View Palette", an Isometric view, and the section view as shown. This is a review of material previously covered. Use "Hidden Line" display mode and "Tangent Edge Removed" for the Front and Section views and "Tangent Edge Visible" for the Isometric.

298. - After adding the "Section" view, we need a close-up of the center of the part. We will add a second Front view using the "**Model View**" command from the View Layout tab and then it will be cropped. The reason for not adding a Detail view is that adding another circle may make the Front view confusing.

From the "Model View" properties, select the *'Worm Gear'* part from the list of currently open files (or Browse to select it) and click in the "Next" arrow at the top to go to the next step.

In the next screen select the Front view from the "Standard views", and leave the "Create multiple views" checkbox cleared, as we only need to add one view; to help us visualize turn on the "Preview" checkbox at the bottom.

Also change the new view to "Hidden Lines Removed" and the scale to 2:1 from the view's PropertyManager.

Move the mouse pointer to the graphics area and locate the new Front view in the upper left corner. Click OK when done. Change the new view to "Tangent Edges Removed."

299. - The second Front view is too big, and since we are only interested in the details of its center we'll crop the view. In order to make a "**Crop View**", first we need to draw a closed profile using regular sketch tools. The closed profile can be anything including circles, rectangles, polygons, ellipses, closed splines, etc. From the Sketch tab in the CommandManager select the "**Ellipse**" icon. To draw an ellipse, click to locate the center and then click to locate the major and minor axes. You'll see the preview as you go. Click OK when finished.

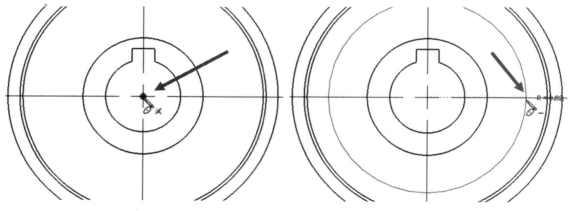

Start the ellipse   Locate major axis

Locate minor axis to finish

300. - Select the ellipse we just drew and click in the "**Crop View**" icon from the View Layout tab. The view will be automatically cropped to the ellipse.

 To change or delete the crop from a view, select the cropped view in the FeatureManager (it will have a scissors icon) and from the right mouse button menu select "**Crop View, Edit Crop**" or "**Remove Crop.**"

301. - Now import the dimensions from the model using "**Model Items.**" Remember to select the options "Import items into all views" and "Entire Model." After importing the dimensions, delete and arrange them (Shift-drag) as needed to match the following image; you may have to change one or more dimensions to display as diameter by right-mouse-clicking it and selecting "**Display Options, Display as Diameter.**"

302. - Now we need to add an angular dimension. To do this click on the "**Smart Dimension**" icon and select the two edges indicated to add the 32° dimension.

SECTION A-A

 To change the dimension's precision (Significant decimal numbers) select the dimension, move the mouse over the "**Dimension Palette**" and change the number of decimal places to "None" from the precision's pull-down menu. Click anywhere outside the Dimension Palette to finish.

SECTION A-A   SECTION A-A

SECTION A-A

303. - The next thing we need to do is to add a "**Chamfer Dimension**." Click in the graphics area with the right mouse button, and from the pop-up menu select "**More Dimensions, Chamfer**", or the menu "**Tools, Dimensions, Chamfer**" or from the "**Smart Dimension**" drop-down icon.

304. - To add a chamfer dimension select the chamfered edge first, then the vertical edge to measure the angle against it, and finally locate the dimension.

305. - We'll finish the Chamfer Dimension by changing the precision for both distance and angle. Select the chamfer dimension, and from the dimension's properties change the "**Tolerance/Precision**" to ".1", this will change the dimension to one decimal place. In the "**2nd Tolerance/Precision**" select "None" to remove the decimal places from the angular value.

We have to do this change in the PropertyManager, because the "**Dimension Palette**" can only change both values to the same precision, and not individually.

306. - In this drawing we are showing the title block. The title block is the area of the drawing where we can communicate important information: add our company name, part number, material, etc. In SolidWorks this is called the "**Sheet Format**." One characteristic of the sheet format is that it is "locked", and we cannot change it directly. To change the title block, right-mouse-click in the drawing area *or* in "*Sheet Format1*" in the Feature Manager and from the pop-up menu select "**Edit Sheet Format**."

307. - After selecting "**Edit Sheet Format**" we are now editing the title block and are free to change it; all the sketch tools are available to modify it as needed. Notice that the drawing views are automatically hidden when editing the "**Sheet Format**." The default sheet format has a few parametric notes that are linked to component properties like the part's name and material, and other notes are linked to the drawing's information like scale and sheet number.

UNLESS OTHERWISE SPECIFIED:		NAME	DATE	TITLE:			
DIMENSIONS ARE IN INCHES	DRAWN						
TOLERANCES: FRACTIONAL±	CHECKED			Gear P/N AB-2468			
ANGULAR: MACH± BEND ± TWO PLACE DECIMAL ±	ENG APPR.						
THREE PLACE DECIMAL ±	MFG APPR.						
INTERPRET GEOMETRIC TOLERANCING PER:	Q.A.			SIZE	DWG. NO.		REV
	COMMENTS:			A	Worm Gear		
MATERIAL AISI 1020							
FINISH							
DO NOT SCALE DRAWING				SCALE: 1:1	WEIGHT: 0.38	SHEET 1 OF 1	

| 3 | 2 | 1 |

308. - Edit the notes by double-clicking them to change the font size and style as needed, and add a new note linked to your name. Note that the "Material", "Weight", "Description" (*Title:*) and the component's name values are filled in automatically from the part's properties, and the scale and sheet number are filled in from the drawing's properties. These parametric notes are in the default sheet format. Change the additional notes to the "Format" layer to match the rest of the Sheet Format notes.

UNLESS OTHERWISE SPECIFIED:		NAME	DATE	**DESIGNER:** Alejandro Reyes			
DIMENSIONS ARE IN INCHES	DRAWN			TITLE:			
TOLERANCES: FRACTIONAL±	CHECKED						
ANGULAR: MACH± BEND ± TWO PLACE DECIMAL ±	ENG APPR.			**Gear P/N AB-2468**			
THREE PLACE DECIMAL ±	MFG APPR.						
INTERPRET GEOMETRIC TOLERANCING PER:	Q.A.			SIZE	DWG. NO.		REV
	COMMENTS:			A	Worm Gear		
MATERIAL AISI 1020							
FINISH							
DO NOT SCALE DRAWING				SCALE: 1:1	WEIGHT: 0.38	SHEET 1 OF 1	

| 3 | 2 | 1 |

After modifying the title block to our liking, exit the sheet format and return to editing the drawing by selecting "**Edit Sheet**" from the right mouse button menu, or clicking in the "**Sheet Format**" confirmation corner.

 If we modify an empty drawing's Sheet Format and save it as a template, the title block changes will be saved with the template and be available for new drawings based on this template. See the Appendix for more information on templates.

309. - Change the reference dimensions (grey) to the "Format" layer to change their color to black, save and close the drawing file.

SECTION A-A

UNLESS OTHERWISE SPECIFIED:			NAME	DATE	DESIGNER: Alejandro Reyes		
DIMENSIONS ARE IN INCHES		DRAWN					
TOLERANCES: FRACTIONAL± ANGULAR: MACH± BEND ± TWO PLACE DECIMAL ± THREE PLACE DECIMAL ±		CHECKED			TITLE:		
		ENG APPR.					
		MFG APPR.			Gear P/N AB-2468		
INTERPRET GEOMETRIC TOLERANCING PER:		QA.					
MATERIAL AISI 1020		COMMENTS:					
					SIZE DWG. NO.		REV
FINISH					A	Worm Gear	
PROPRIETARY AND CONFIDENTIAL THE INFORMATION CONTAINED IN THIS DRAWING IS THE SOLE PROPERTY OF <INSERT COMPANY NAME HERE>. ANY REPRODUCTION IN PART OR AS A WHOLE WITHOUT THE WRITTEN PERMISSION OF <INSERT COMPANY NAME HERE> IS PROHIBITED.							
NEXT ASSY	USED ON				SCALE: 1:1	WEIGHT: 0.38	SHEET 1 OF 1
APPLICATION		DO NOT SCALE DRAWING					

Exercises: Make the detail drawing of the following Engine Project parts that were done in the Part Modeling section to match the drawings previously supplied to make each part. High resolution images at mechanicad.com.

Connecting Rod	Crankshaft
Con Rod Crankshaft Half Bushing	Bushing Top Con Rod
Oil Seal	Pin ConRod-Piston

Notes:

Drawing Six: The Worm Gear Shaft

Notes:

Just as we did with the *'Offset Shaft'* drawing, we'll reinforce making new drawings, adding views, importing dimensions, moving dimensions from one view to another and changing a diameter's display style. In this exercise we will make Left, Front and Top views, import and arrange the model dimensions and learn how to make a new type of view called "**Broken-Out Section**" to complete the drawing.

310. - Open the *'Worm Gear Shaft'* part and add Material, Weight, Description ("*Shaft with hex drive*") and "MyName" custom properties. Make a new drawing using the "A-Landscape" drawing template. Add the Front view from the View Palette, click above it to add a Top view, and to the left to add the Left view. Use "Hidden Lines Removed" mode for all 3 views. Change the sheet scale to 1:1. Edit the Sheet Format to change the note's font size to fit.

311. - Import the dimensions from the model…

312. -…and arrange them.

313. - One more thing we need to add to the drawing is a centerline. SolidWorks allows us to add a centerline to every cylindrical face of the model. To add centerlines to our drawing views, select the "**Centerline**" icon from the Annotation Tab, and click in the cylindrical surface that we need to add a centerline to. When finished adding centerlines click OK to finish.

314. - Instead of changing the Front view display to "Hidden Lines Visible" to see the details of the keyway, we will make a "**Broken-Out Section**" view. What the broken out section does is to cut-out a region to a specific depth to reveal details otherwise hidden. Select the "**Broken-Out Section**" icon from the "View Layout" tab, and similar to the "Detail" view where we get a circle tool to define it, in the Broken-out-Section we get a "**Spline**" to define the region to cut. A Spline is a very smooth polynomial curve connected by multiple points. Draw the following "**Spline**" approximately as shown by clicking to locate the points that will define the curve. Splines can be open or closed, in our case the last point will be coincident to the first one to make a closed spline.

If we want to define the region for the Broken-Out Section using a different tool, such as lines, arcs or ellipses, draw a closed profile using those tools and pre-select it before activating the **"Broken-Out Section"** tool.

315. - When the last point of the **Spline** is added, we get the **"Broken-Out Section"** properties, where we are asked to enter a depth to make the cut or select an edge of the model to define the depth. Select the vertical edge indicated in the Top view to define how deep the cut will be. By selecting the vertical edge the depth is set to its midpoint making the cut go to the center of the part.

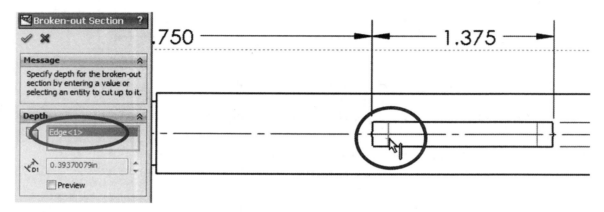

Click OK to finish the Broken-out Section.

To edit or delete the **"Broken-Out Section"**, right-mouse-click <u>inside</u> the section's region and from the **"Broken-Out Section"** menu select "Delete", "Edit Definition" (to change its depth) or "Edit Sketch" to modify the cut-out area.

316. - In this drawing, it may be a good idea to manually add a reference dimension for the hexagonal cut. To show the construction circle we can make the sketch for the hexagonal cut visible. Expand the view in the FeatureManager, right-mouse-click in the cut's sketch and select "Show" from the pop-up menu. Save the drawing and close the file.

Exercises: Make the detail drawing of the following Engine Project parts that were done in the Part Modeling section to match the drawings previously supplied for each part. These will complete the Engine Project drawings. High resolution images at mechanicad.com.

Internal Retaining Ring

Retaining Ring Crankshaft Bearing

Exhaust

Oil Dip Stick

Engine Block

Piston Head

Oil Pan

Crank Case Top

Extra Credit: Using the parts made for the gas grill project make the corresponding detail drawings. The finished components can be downloaded from our website:

http://mechanicad.com/download.html

Notes:

Assembly Modeling

The next step in the design after making the parts and drawings is to get all the parts together into an assembly. The process of designing the parts first and then assembling them is known as "Bottom-Up Design." This is similar to buying a bicycle; when you open the box, you get all the pieces needed ready for assembly. A different approach, usually known as "Top-Down Design" is where the parts are designed while working in the assembly; this is a very powerful tool that allows us to match parts to each other, changing a part if another component is modified. In this book we'll cover the Bottom-Up Design technique, since it is easier to understand and is also the basis for the advanced Top-Down Design, which is covered in the **Beginner's Guide to SolidWorks Level II** book. In general, it's a good idea to design the parts, make the assembly to make sure everything fits and works as expected (Form, Fit and Function), and *then* make the drawings of the parts and assemblies; this way the drawings are done at the end, when you are sure everything works correctly.

So far, we've been working on parts, single components that are the building blocks of an assembly. In an assembly we have multiple components, either parts or other assemblies (in this case called subassemblies.) The way we tell SolidWorks how to relate components (parts and/or subassemblies) together is by using Mates or relations between them. Mates in the assembly are similar to the geometric relations in the sketch, but in the assembly we reference faces, planes, edges, axes, vertices and even sketch geometry from the features in the components in order to align them to each other.

In an assembly, the components are added one at a time until we complete the design. In an assembly every component has six degrees of freedom, meaning that they can move and rotate six different ways: three translations along the X, Y and Z axes, and three rotations about the X, Y and Z axes. By mating components to each other we are essentially restricting how they move in relation to one another based on which degrees of freedom are constrained. This is the basis for assembly motion and simulation.

The first component we add to the assembly has all six degrees of freedom fixed by default. Therefore, it's a good idea that the first component added to the assembly is one that will be a reference for the rest of the components. For example, if we make a bicycle assembly, the first component added to the assembly would be the frame. For the gear box we are designing, the first component added to the assembly will be the *'Housing'* as the rest of the components will be attached to it.

Notes:

The Gear Housing Assembly

Notes:

In making the *'Gear Housing'* assembly, we will learn many assembly tools and operations, including making new assemblies, adding components, adding Mating relations between them and adding fasteners. We'll cover component design tables, interference detection, assembly exploded views and how to change a part's dimensions while working in the assembly. The sequence to follow while making the *'Gear Housing'* assembly is the following:

New Assembly	Add the Housing; change configuration	Add and mate the first Side Cover	Add and mate the second Side Cover
Add and mate the Worm Gear Shaft	Change component colors	Add and mate the Worm Gear	Add and mate the Offset Shaft
Add and mate the Top Cover	Add screws	Find interferences and correct them	Make exploded view

317. - The first thing we need to do to make a new assembly is to select the **"New"** document icon, select the Assembly template and click on OK.

318. - The first thing we see when we make a new assembly is the "**Begin Assembly**" dialog to start adding components. As we discussed previously, the *'Housing'* will be the first component added. Click "Browse" to locate the *'Housing'* part file, select it in the "**Open**" dialog box making sure we are using the *"Machined"* configuration in the "Configurations" drop-down menu. If you cannot see the component that you want, make sure you are looking in the correct folder and have the "**Files of Type**" set to *"Part"* in the "Quick Filter." Click "**Open**" when done. If you have the "Graphics Preview" option box checked, you will see a preview of the component being inserted.

319. - After selecting the *'Housing'* we have to locate it in the assembly; when we move the mouse the part's preview follows it. What we want to do is to locate the *'Housing'* at the assembly origin. If you cannot see the assembly origin (which is hidden in the default assembly template), turn it on by selecting the menu "**View, Origins**" (this can be done while you are inserting a component.) The reason to locate the *'Housing'* at the assembly's origin is to have the *'Housing's* planes and origin aligned with the assembly's planes and origin. To add the *'Housing'* AND align it with the assembly's origin, click the OK button *or* move the mouse pointer to the assembly origin and click on it. (The cursor will have a double origin next to it and you will see the *'Housing'* "snap" in place before clicking.)

346

320. - If the *'Housing'* is loaded by mistake showing the *"Forge"* configuration, do not worry, as it can be changed by selecting the "*Housing*" part in the FeatureManager and clicking "Component Properties" from the pop-up toolbar.

 If the component added to the assembly has configurations, the selected configuration is shown next to the part's name in the FeatureManager in parentheses.

From the **"Referenced Configuration"** box, select the *"Machined"* configuration and click on OK. The *'Housing'* in the graphics area should now show the *"Machined"* configuration.

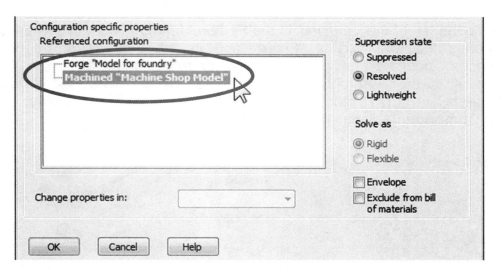

321. - Once in the Assembly environment, the toolbars are changed in the CommandManager; now we have an Assembly tab. Also notice at the bottom of the Assembly FeatureManager a special folder called **"Mates**." This is where the relations between components (Mates) will be stored.

322. - To the left of the *'Housing'* in the FeatureManager, we can see a letter "**f**"; this means that the part is "**Fixed**" and its six degrees of freedom are constrained, meaning that it cannot move or rotate about any axis. The first component in the assembly is always automatically fixed and subsequent components are not. To add the second component to our assembly, click the "**Insert Components**" icon in the Assembly tab…

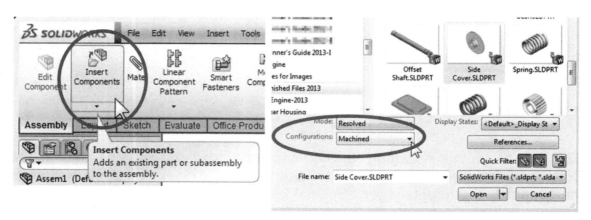

…browse to the folder where *'Side Cover'* was saved and open it. As with the *'Housing'*, make sure we also select the "Machined" configuration before opening the *'Side Cover'*.

323. - Place the *'Side Cover'* next to the *'Housing'* as seen in the next image. Don't worry about the exact location; we'll locate it accurately next using mates.

324. - After adding the *'Side Cover'* part, it's name in the FeatureManager is preceded by a (-), this means that the part has <u>at least</u> one unconstrained degree of freedom. Since this part was just inserted, all six degrees of freedom are unconstrained and the part is free to move in any direction and rotate about all three axes.

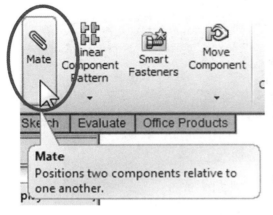

325. - Now we are ready to add the relations (Mates) between the *'Housing'* and the *'Side Cover'*. The mates will help us reference one component to another, locating and restricting their motion. As explained earlier, mates can be added between faces, planes, edges, vertices, axes and even sketch geometry. Click on the **"Mate"** icon in the Assembly tab or select the menu **"Insert, Mate"** to locate the *'Side Cover'* on the *'Housing'*.

 Whenever possible, select model faces as your first option for mates, faces are easier to select and visualize most of the time.

326. - For the first mate, select the two <u>cylindrical faces</u> indicated in the next picture.

As soon as the second face is selected, SolidWorks recognizes that both faces are cylindrical and automatically "snaps" them with a **Concentric mate**. (SolidWorks defaults to concentric as it is the most logical option.) The *'Side Cover'* is the part that moves because it is the part with unconstrained degrees of freedom; remember the *'Housing'* was fixed when it was inserted, and therefore, it cannot move. In this case the **Concentric mate** is pre-selected; click the OK button in the pop-up toolbar to add this mate.

327. - Note the pop-up toolbar shows options to mate the entities. (These options are listed in the PropertyManager, too.) This toolbar helps us to be more productive by minimizing mouse travel. The following table shows the basic mate options available:

Standard Mates	Entities that can be mated
Coincident	Two Faces, Planes, Edges, Vertices, Axes, Sketch points/endpoints, or any combination.
Parallel	Two flat Faces, Planes, linear Edges, Axes or any combination.
Perpendicular	Two flat Faces, Planes, Edges, Axes or any combination.
Tangent	Two cylindrical Faces; one flat Face and one cylindrical; a cylindrical Face and one linear Edge.
Concentric	Two cylindrical Faces, two round Edges, two linear Edges or Axes, one cylindrical Face and one round Edge, one cylindrical Face and one linear Edge.
Lock	This option constrains all degrees of freedom of the component, locking it in place.
1.00in ☑ Flip dimension	Specify a distance between any two valid entities for Coincident or Parallel mates. "Flip dimension" reverses the direction to one side or the other. Using this mate on two flat Faces or Planes will also make them parallel.
☐ Flip dimension 0.00deg	Specify an angle between any two valid entities for Coincident, Parallel or Concentric mates. "Flip dimension" will reverse the direction of the angular dimension.
Mate alignment: ___or	Reverses the orientation of the components being mated. For two Faces, to look at each other or away.

328. - After adding the first mate, the dialog remains visible, this means that we are ready to add more mates. It will remain active until we click **Cancel** or hit "Esc" on the keyboard. Notice that the mate added is listed under the "**Mates**" box in the PropertyManager. We'll continue adding mates at this time; do not exit the "**Mate**" command.

329. - For the second mate, select the two cylindrical faces indicated (one from the *'Side Cover'*, and one from the *'Housing'*.) SolidWorks defaults again to a **Concentric** mate and rotates the *'Side Cover'* to align the holes; this will prevent the *'Side Cover'* from rotating. We can use the **"Magnifying Glass"** to make selection of small faces easier. Click OK to add the mate. *IF* the *'Side Cover'* is *inside* the *'Housing'*, click-and-drag it with the left mouse button to get it out and allow us to add the remaining mates.

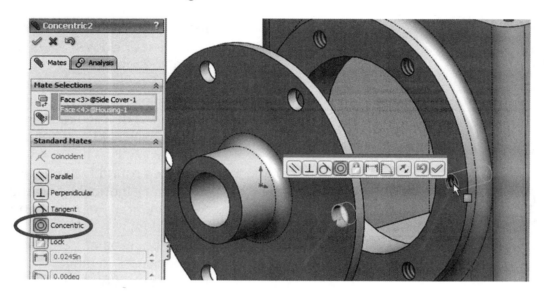

In this case the Concentric mate works as expected because the holes are located <u>exactly</u> at the same distance from the center in both parts; in reality, it is generally a better idea to align the two components using Planes and/or Faces, with either a Parallel or Coincident mate, as will be done in a few more steps.

330. - The last mate will be a **Coincident mate** between the back face of the *'Side Cover'* and the front face of the *'Housing'*; use **"Select Other"** or rotate the view to select the faces if needed (If the *'Side Cover'* is <u>inside</u> the *'Housing'*, click-and-drag to move it out.) The cover will move to make the faces touch; the **Coincident mate** will be pre-selected. Click OK to add the mate and finish the "Mate" command by either clicking OK, Cancel or pressing the "Esc" key.

Using the "**Select Other**" tool will allow you us to select hidden component faces without having to rotate the view.

331. - All six degrees of freedom of the *'Side Cover'* have now been constrained using mates; this can be seen in the FeatureManager where the *'Side Cover'* is no longer preceded by a (-) sign. Notice that the "**Mates**" folder now includes the two Concentric and one Coincident mate we just added; SolidWorks adds the names of the mated components in each mate for reference. Changing the width of the FeatureManager we can see the component's names.

 IMPORTANT: *If a (+) sign precedes a part name, you probably also received an error message telling you that the assembly had been **over defined**. If this is the case, it means you added conflicting mates that cannot be solved, or inadvertently selected the wrong faces or edges when adding mates.*

*The easiest way to correct this error is to either hit the **Undo** button or delete the last mate in the "Mates" folder; you will be able to identify the conflicting mate because it will have an error icon next to it. If multiple mates have errors, start deleting the last mate at the bottom (this is the last one added); chances are, this is the cause of the problem. If you still have errors, keep deleting mates with errors from the bottom up until you clear all the errors. It's not a good idea to proceed with errors, as it will only get worse.*

332. - We are now ready to add the second *'Side Cover'* to our assembly. Repeat the "**Insert Component**" command to add a second *'Side Cover'* and locate it on the other side of the *'Housing'* as shown. Remember to use the "Machined" configuration. Don't worry too much about the exact location, in the next step we'll move and rotate the part.

 A quick way to add a copy of a component already in the assembly is to hold down the "Ctrl" key and click-and-drag the part to be copied within the assembly.

333. - When the second *'Side Cover'* is inserted, it has a (-) sign next to it in the FeatureManager; remember, this means that it has <u>at least</u> one unconstrained Degree of Freedom (DOF). Since this part was just inserted in the assembly, all six DOF are unconstrained, and the component can be moved and rotated. To "**Move**" a component, click-and-drag it with the <u>left mouse button</u>. To "**Rotate**" it, click-and-drag it with the <u>right mouse button</u>. "Move" and "Rotate" the second *'Side Cover'* as needed to align it *approximately* as shown. Remember, we'll add more mates to locate it precisely. Turn off the "Origins" (menu "View, Origins") and rotate the view as we did with parts to view the assembly from the back.

334. - We will now add three mates to the second cover as we did to the first *'Side Cover'*. Select the "Mate" icon from the Assembly tab and add a **Concentric** mate selecting the faces indicated. Rotate the view (not the part) to get a better view of the faces to select. Optionally as a shortcut we can select one of the faces to be mated, and from the pop-up toolbar, select the "**Mate**" icon.

 Before adding the second Concentric mate, click-and-drag the cover. Notice that it can rotate about its center and also move along the axis; under-constrained components are the basis for SolidWorks to simulate motion.

335. - Now add the Concentric mate to align the screw holes between the *'Side Cover'* and the *'Housing'*. Since the part is symmetrical, it doesn't really matter which two holes are selected. If the cover had a feature that needed to be aligned, then orientating the part correctly would be important.

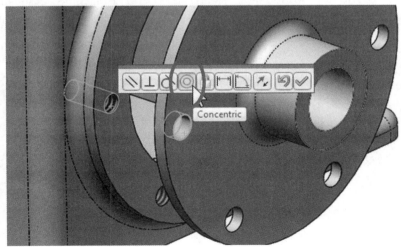

336. - Finally add a Coincident mate between the flat face of the *'Housing'* and the second *'Side Cover'* as we did with the first cover. Use **"Select Other"** to select the hidden face, or rotate the part. Click OK to continue.

337. - It is very important to notice that these mates could have been added in any order; we chose this order to make it easier for the reader to see the effect of each mate on each part. Whichever order you select, you will end up with both *'Side Cover'* parts fully defined (no free DOF) and six mates in the "Mates" folder as listed next.

Origin
(f) Housing<1> (Machined<<Default>_Display S
Side Cover<1> (Machined<<Default>_Display St
Side Cover<2> (Machined<<Default>_Display St
Mates
　Concentric1 (Housing<1>,Side Cover<1>)
　Concentric2 (Housing<1>,Side Cover<1>)
　Coincident1 (Housing<1>,Side Cover<1>)
　Concentric3 (Housing<1>,Side Cover<2>)
　Concentric4 (Housing<1>,Side Cover<2>)
　Coincident2 (Housing<1>,Side Cover<2>)

338. - Now that we have correctly mated both *'Side Covers'*, we'll add the *'Worm Gear Shaft'* using the same procedure as before and locate it somewhere above the *'Housing'*.

339. - With four different components in the assembly, it's a good idea to change their appearance to identify them easily. To change a component's color, select the component in the FeatureManager or the graphics screen, and from the pop-up toolbar select the "**Appearance**" icon. From the drop-down list, select the first option to change the part's color at the assembly level only. This means that the color will change only in the assembly and not in the part file. The second option will change the part's color at the part level.

We can change a part's appearance in the assembly, or in the part file. Picture it like this: We can paint the part *before* we assemble it, or we paint it *after* we assemble it. In the second case, the part color changes only after it has been assembled, and in the second case we assemble a painted part. For this example, we want to change the color at the assembly level, which is the option indicated above.

340. - We are now ready to change the part's color. Select the desired color from the color swatch selection box to change it. Click OK to finish.

341. - Change the color of both covers to your liking and continue adding mates. (It does look better in color!)

342. - Since we covered **Concentric** and **Coincident** mates and practiced them with the *'Side Covers'*, rotate the *'Shaft'* approximately as shown in the first image and add a Concentric and a Coincident mate using the faces indicated.

Concentric mate

Coincident mate

Notice that the *'Worm Gear Shaft'* is not yet fully defined; it still has a (-)sign before its name in the FeatureManager. In this case the only DOF left unconstrained is to rotate about its axis, and that is exactly what we want; the *'Worm Gear Shaft'* is supposed to rotate. If we click-and-drag it, we'll see it rotate. (Look at the keyway while rotating it.)

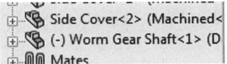

343. - The next component to be added will be the *'Worm Gear'*. Add it with the **"Insert Component"** command as before and place it in the assembly as shown. And now that you know how, change its color too.

344. - To mate the *'Worm Gear'* in place, select the "**Mate**" icon and add a Concentric mate with the *'Worm Gear Shaft'* using the cylindrical inside face of the *'Worm Gear'* and the outside face of the *'Worm Gear Shaft'*. After adding this mate, drag the *'Worm Gear'* and note how it moves along the shaft and rotates about it.

345. - Now we need to center the *'Worm Gear'* inside the *'Housing'*. To do this we can use the *'Worm Gear's'* "*Front Plane*" and the "*Front Plane*" of the *'Housing'* or the assembly, which are conveniently located in the center of the *'Housing'*. (Remember we made the *'Housing'* symmetrical about the origin? ☺)

Select the **Mate** command (if it's not open already) and add a **Coincident** mate selecting the "*Front Plane*" of the *'Housing'* (or the assembly) and the "*Front Plane*" of the *'Worm Gear'* from the fly-out FeatureManager. Expand the parts' feature trees to select their planes. In the following image the 'Worm Gear' was moved outside for visibility purposes.

After adding this mate, the *'Worm Gear'* is still under defined, and we want the *'Worm Gear Shaft'* and the *'Worm Gear'* to rotate together. To accomplish this, we'll have to add either a **Coincident** mate using the corresponding planes from the parts, or a **Parallel** mate between the faces of the keyways. We'll add the Parallel mate in this step and let the reader explore the other option.

346. - As luck would have it, the *'Housing'* is obstructing the view to the keyways, and we'll need to hide it in order to add the next mate. Cancel the **"Mate"** command; select the *'Housing'* in the FeatureManger or in the graphics area, and select the **"Hide/Show"** icon from the pop-up toolbar. The part will be hidden, allowing us to see the rest of the components to add the next mate. After we are done mating the parts we'll make it visible again.

347. - As soon as we hide the part, it disappears from the screen and we can see inside without obstructions. The *'Housing'* icon in the FeatureManager changes to white, this is how we know that the part is hidden.

348. - Select the **"Mate"** icon again and select the flat faces of the *'Worm Gear Shaft'* and *'Worm Gear'* keyways. In this case, we'll use a **Parallel** mate. The reason for choosing a **Parallel mate** is because it can absorb small dimensional differences that may exist between the parts preventing them from being exactly coincident, and making the parallel gives us the desired result. In general this is a more forgiving option. Click OK to add the mate and close the "Mate" command.

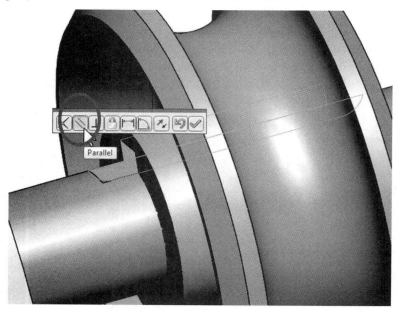

After adding the mate, click-and-drag the *'Worm Gear'* or the *'Worm Gear Shaft'*, see how both of them move at the same time, as if they had a keyway.

Extra credit: Build a keyway and add it to the assembly, mating the keyway to the *'Worm Gear Shaft'*, and the *'Worm Gear'* to the keyway.

349. - To show the *'Housing'* again we'll reverse the process that we used to hide it. Select the *'Housing'* from the FeatureManager and select the **"Hide/Show Component"** icon from the pop-up toolbar. This command is really a toggle switch. If a component is hidden, it will show it; if the component is visible, it will hide it.

350. - Now add the *'Offset Shaft'* to the assembly and mate it in place. Insert the *'Offset Shaft'* using the "**Insert Component**" command and change its color for visibility.

351. - Add mates by selecting one of the model faces to be mated, and from the pop-up toolbar, select the "**Mate**" icon. When the "**Mate**" command is displayed, the model face is already selected and we only need to select the other face to add a Concentric mate.

352. - Now we need a Coincident mate to prevent the shaft from moving along its axis. We'll use the groove in the *'Shaft'* for this mate. In this case, we can use either the flat face or the edge of the groove; selecting the edge may be easier than selecting the face. We can use the "**Magnifying Glass**" tool to zoom in and make our selections. Click OK to finish the mate.

353. - The last component we're adding is the *'Top Cover'*. Add it to the assembly and, if you wish, change its color. First add a **Concentric** mate to align one of the holes of the cover to the corresponding hole in the *'Housing'*. For this mate, you can use either faces or circular edges; it will work the same. An interesting detail to notice is that, when we add a Concentric mate, it removes four DOF from the component: two translations and two rotations when mated to a fixed or fully defined reference.

354. - Check the remaining two DOF by dragging the *'Top Cover'* with the left mouse button; it will rotate and move up and down. By adding a Coincident mate between the *bottom face* of the *'Top Cover'* and the *top face* of the *'Housing'*, we'll remove one more DOF.

355. - If we now click-and-drag the *'Top Cover'*, it will turn; now we only have one DOF left. To finish constraining the *'Top Cover'* we'll add a **Parallel** mate between the *'Top Cover'* and *'Housing'*. As we explained earlier, the reason for the Parallel mate is that sometimes components don't match exactly, and if we add a Coincident mate, we may be forcing a condition that cannot be met, over defining the assembly and getting an error message. The Parallel mate can be added between Faces, Planes and/or Edges. In this particular case, we can use either a Coincident or Parallel mate since the parts were designed to match exactly. However, in real life they may not; that's why we chose a Parallel mate.

Your assembly should now look like this.

SmartMates

SmartMates are a quick and easy way to add certain mate types between components simply by dragging parts or assemblies onto each other using flat, cylindrical or conical faces, circular or linear edges, vertices or temporary axes. The basic idea is to hold down the "Alt" key while we drag the face, edge or vertex of the component to be mated *onto* the face, edge or vertex of the other component.

We'll re-create the entire assembly up to this point using the SmartMates approach, now that the concept of mates has been explained and we have a better idea of the general process. The next table shows the types of SmartMates available and their corresponding feedback icon when used.

 When SmartMates is enabled the icon will change to a clip attached to the face, edge or vertex being dragged.

Entities to be mated/ Feedback icon	Resulting Mate
2 Flat Faces	**Coincident Faces**
2 Linear Edges	**Coincident Edges**

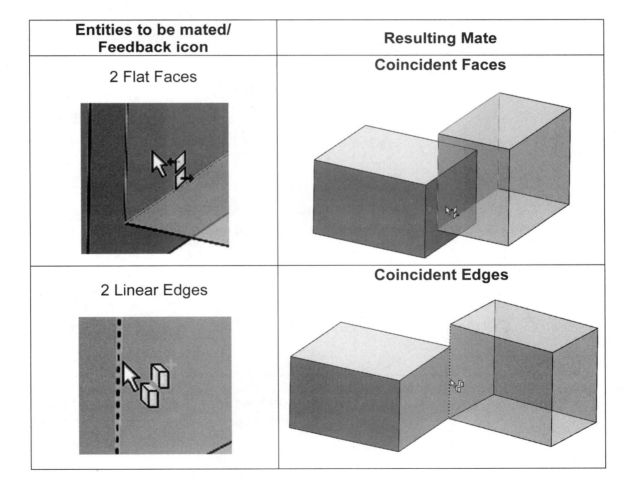

Entities to be mated/ Feedback icon	Resulting Mate
2 Cylindrical / Conical Faces	**Concentric**
2 Round Edges	**Peg-in-Hole** (Adds 1 Concentric mate between the cylindrical/conical faces and 1 Coincident Mate between the flat faces)
2 vertices	**Coincident Vertices**

 When using SmartMates to mate two flanged faces, SolidWorks will add a Peg-in-Hole mate and an extra Concentric mate between two holes in the flanged faces to align them.

356. - Let's recreate the entire assembly now using SmartMates. An alternate way to start an assembly is similar to the way we made the detail drawings. Open the *'Housing'* part, and from the **"New"** document icon select **"Make Assembly from Part/Assembly"**, or the menu **"File, Make Assembly from Part."** Make sure the selected configuration is "Machined" before making the assembly. Just as we did previously, add the '*Housing*' at the origin. If you cannot see the origin, turn it on in the menu "**View, Origins**."

357. - Now, bring in the *'Side Cover'* with the **"Insert Component"** command and put it next to the *'Housing'* with the "Machined" configuration, just as we did before up to this point.

358. - Now we can start using the SmartMates functionality. Press and hold the "**Alt**" key on the keyboard and, while holding it down, left-click-and-drag the *'Side Cover'* from the edge indicated. Notice that as soon as we start moving it, the "Mate" icon appears next to the mouse pointer, and the *'Side Cover'* becomes transparent.

359. - Keep dragging the *'Side Cover'* until we touch the flat face or the round edge in the front face of the *'Housing'*; at this time the *'Side Cover'* will 'snap' into place and will give us the "**Peg-in-Hole**" mate icon. Release the mouse button to finish. The *'Side Cover'* is now fully defined to the *'Housing'* with a single step.

Expanding the "Mates" folder in the FeatureManager, we can see that two Concentric mates and one Coincident mate have been added. Select the mates to see the faces that were automatically mated in each one.

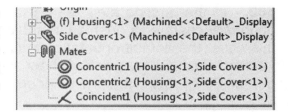

360. - We can mate the second *'Side Cover'* easily with SmartMates, but in this step we'll show how to add it by using the "**Mirror Components**" command. Select the menu "**Insert, Mirror Components**."

361. - Similar to the "Mirror Feature" command, we need a plane or flat face to be used as a Mirror Plane. In this case, we can select the assembly's "*Front Plane*" as the Mirror Plane (since it is located in the middle of the assembly), and in the "Components to Mirror" selection box, select the *'Side Cover'*. After making your selections, click on the "Next" blue arrow to go to the next step in the "**Mirror Component**" command.

371

362. - In the second step we get a preview of the mirrored part and we can optionally change its orientation and/or create an "opposite hand" version of it. In this case, the default orientation is correct and we don't need an opposite hand version. Click OK to finish. A new instance of the *'Side Cover'* is added and a *"Mirror Component"* feature is added to the FeatureManager.

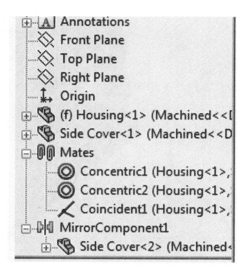

363. - Another way to add parts to an assembly is by dragging them directly from *Windows Explorer*. Open the folder where we have the part files stored and drag-and-drop the *'Worm Gear Shaft'* directly into the assembly window.

364. - After adding the *'Worm Gear Shaft'* to the assembly, rotate it to a position that will allow us to view both of the edges that we want to mate using the right-mouse-button click-and-drag method. SmartMates has a limitation, in the sense that we need to be able to see both of the mate references for it to work, in this case the edge indicated in the left image and the *'Side Cover'* center hole. Hold down the "Alt" key, then click-and-drag the *Worm Gear Shaft's* edge to the *'Side Cover'* to add a "Peg-in-Hole" SmartMate.

365. - Another way to add a component to an assembly is by opening it in SolidWorks, arranging the part and assembly windows side by side (menu "**Window, Tile Vertically**"), and dragging the part into the assembly. In this version of the assembly we'll use the '*Worm Gear Complete*', it will help us visualize a new type of mate later on. One advantage of adding components using this approach is that dragging the part using the face that we want to mate into the assembly activates the SmartMates function automatically.

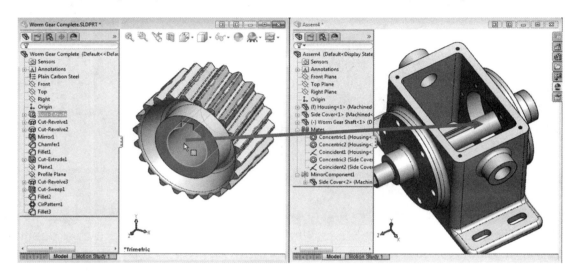

366. - As we drag the '*Worm Gear*' into the assembly window, move the part to the outside face of the '*Worm Gear Shaft*' to add a Concentric mate automatically using SmartMates (look for the Concentric mate icon.) Select OK in the pop-up toolbar after dropping the '*Worm Gear*' to add the mate.

We can drag parts into assemblies using faces, edges or vertices, just as we would when using SmartMates. The only difference is that we don't have to press the "Alt" key while dragging from a part (or assembly) window into an assembly window.

367. - The next step is to center the *'Worm Gear Complete'* inside the *'Housing'*. In the previous assembly we added a mate using the part's and assembly's planes. In this case we'll use a new mate called "**Width**." Maximize the assembly window, select the "**Mate**" command, expand the "**Advanced Mates**" section and select "**Width**." In the "Width selections:" select the two inside faces of the *'Housing'*; click in the "Tab selections:" box and select the two outside flat faces of the *'Worm Gear'* (the small round faces.) The *'Worm Gear Complete'* will be automatically centered. The function of the "**Width**" mate centers the "Tab" selections between the "Width" selections. Click OK to finish. After adding the "Width" mate don't forget to add the parallel mate between the keyway.

375

368. - Add the *'Offset Shaft Gear'* to the assembly and add a "Peg-in-Hole" mate using SmartMates using the indicated edge.

369. - Add the *'Top Cover'* using any of the methods learned so far, and flip it upside down as shown in the next picture using a right mouse button click-and-drag. The reason to flip it is to allow us to see both edges (needed for a SmartMate) to show how to flip the direction of a SmartMate.

370. - Select the edge indicated, and add a **Peg-in-Hole** SmartMate. Note that the *'Top Cover'* may be upside down in the preview. **WHILE STILL PRESSING THE LEFT MOUSE BUTTON** to add the mate, release the "Alt" key, and press the "Tab" key once; notice how the preview changes flipping the *'Top Cover'* (Pressing the "Tab" key again will flip the mate again.) Make sure you have the correct orientation for the *'Top Cover'* before releasing the left mouse button to add the SmartMate.

One possible orientation…

Orientation after pressing the "Tab" key

371. - Now add the final mate to the *'Top Cover'*. Hold down the "Alt" key and drag the edge of the *'Top Cover'* to the face (or the edge) of the *'Housing'* to make them Coincident. Adding this mate will fully define the *'Top Cover'*. Change the color of the parts as before for easier visualization.

NOTE: The rest of the illustrations will be made using the parts with the gears, but the reader is free to continue either way.

After finishing the same assembly using SmartMates, the reader can see why it's a good idea to learn how to use them, as it speeds up the assembly process making it easier and faster, making us more efficient designers.

Fasteners

The commercial versions of SolidWorks Office Professional and Premium, as well as the Educational Edition available to schools include a library of hardware called "SolidWorks Toolbox" which includes nuts, bolts, screws, pins, washers, bearings, bushings, structural steel, gears, etc. in both metric and imperial units standards.

372. - The "SolidWorks Toolbox" is an accessory that has to be loaded through the menu "**Tools, Add-ins**." For it to work correctly, we have to load both "SolidWorks Toolbox" and "SolidWorks Toolbox Browser."

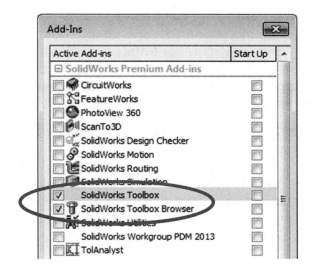

With the "SolidWorks Toolbox", we can add hardware to our assemblies by simply dragging and dropping components, and SolidWorks will automatically add the necessary mates, saving us time. To make it even more powerful and versatile, we can add our own hardware.

373. - To access "SolidWorks Toolbox" we use the **Design Library**, which is located in a tab in the Task Pane. If the Task Pane is not visible, go to the menu "**View, Toolbars, Task Pane**" to activate it.

The "SolidWorks Toolbox" <u>was not included in the</u> *Student Design Kit* as of the writing of this book.

Clicking on the "Design Library" icon opens a fly-out pane that reveals the libraries. The "Design Library" contains four main areas:

- **Design Library**, which includes built-in and user defined libraries of annotations, features and parts that can be dragged and dropped into parts, drawings and assemblies.

- **Toolbox**, which we just described.

- **3D Content Central**, an internet based library of user uploaded and manufacturer certified components, including nuts, bolts and screws, pneumatics, mold and die components, conveyors, bearings, electronic components, industrial hardware, power transmission, piping, automation components, furniture, human models, etc., all available for drag and drop use. All that is needed to access it is an internet connection.

- **SolidWorks Content** allows the user to download weldments libraries, piping, blocks, structural members, etc.

As we can see, the "Design Library" offers a valuable resource for the designer, helping us save time modeling components that are usually purchased or standard, and in the case of the Supplier Certified library, components accurately modeled for use in our designs.

374. - To add screws to our assembly, select the "Design Library" from the Task Pane and click in the (+) sign to the left of the "Toolbox" to expand it.

375. - After expanding the "Toolbox" we can see the many options available. Depending on how "Toolbox" is configured, some standards may not be available. In this exercise we'll use "ANSI Inch, Bolts and Screws" and select "Socket Head Screws."

When we click the "Socket Head Screws" folder, we see in the lower half of the Design Library pane the available styles, including Button Head, Socket Head, Countersunk and Shoulder Screws. For our assembly, we'll use "Socket Head Cap Screws (SHCS)."

376. - First, we want to add the #6-32 screws to the *'Top Cover'*. From the bottom pane of the "Toolbox", click-and-drag the "Socket Head Cap Screw" into one of the holes in the *'Top Cover'*. You will see a transparent preview of the screw and when we get close to the edge of a hole, SolidWorks will automatically snap the screw in place using SmartMates. When we get the preview of the screw assembled where we want it, release the left mouse button. If we release the mouse button before, the screw will still be created, but it will not be automatically assembled or add any mates.

 Do not worry if the preview in your screen is big. When we drop the screw in place, it will size to match the hole.

Notice that the Design Library hides away as soon as we drag the screw into the assembly; this is an automatic feature, unless the user pressed the "stay visible" thumb tack on the upper right of the Task Pane.

Auto-hide On   Always visible

377. - As soon as we drop the screw in the hole, we are presented with a dialog box asking us to select the screw parameters and a pop-up menu where we can select the screw size. In this case, we need a #6-32 screw, 0.5″ long with Hex Drive and Schematic Thread Display. If needed, a part number can be added at the time the fastener is made.

A word on Thread Display options: The Schematic Thread Display will add a revolved cut to the screw to simulate a thread for visual effect. Helical threads can be added as a feature using a sweep, as we saw earlier, but it's generally considered a waste of computer resources. If we had tens or hundreds or even thousands of fasteners in an assembly it would certainly slow down the system noticeably without really adding value to a design in most instances. Helical threads are a resource intensive feature that is best left for times when the helical thread itself is a part of the design and not just for cosmetic reasons. The revolved cut gives a good appearance for most practical purposes and is a simple enough feature that doesn't noticeably affect the PC's performance.

 Toolbox components are stored in a master file that includes the different configurations of each screw type in the Toolbox data folder. If the assembly files are copied to a different computer, the screws used in the assembly will be created there. If the other computer does not have Toolbox, the user can copy all the files using the menu "**File, Pack and go**" to copy all the files used in the assembly, including Toolbox components and component drawings.

378. - After selecting OK from the screw size options box, the screw is created with the selected parameters and mated in the hole where it was dropped. At this point we are ready to add more screws of the same size, if needed. In our example, we'll click in the other 3 holes of the *'Top Cover'* to add the rest of the screws. Notice the graphic preview of the screw as we move the mouse, when we get close to a hole the screw snaps adding a Peg-in-Hole SmartMate. Click "Cancel" to finish adding screws.

379. - We will now add the *'¼-20 Socket Head Cap Screw'* to the *'Side Covers'*. Open the "Design Library" tab and just as the previous step drag and drop the "Socket Head Cap Screw" to one hole of the *'Side Cover'*, but be careful to "drop" the screw in the correct location. If you look closely, there are two different edges where you can insert the screw: one is in the *'Side Cover'*, and the other is in the *'Housing'*. The screw will be mated to the hole you "drop" the screw in. Use the snap preview to help you find the correct one.

380. - After we drop the screw, the screw properties box is displayed. Select the ¼-20, 0.5″ long screw with Hex Drive and Schematic Thread Display. Click OK to build the screw and mate it in the hole where we dropped it and close the "Configure Component" command, we are adding a single screw in this step.

381. - Instead of manually adding the rest of the screws, we'll make a component pattern using the previous screw. Just like with feature patterns in a part, we can add linear or circular patterns of parts, but we also have a special type of pattern that allows us to make a *pattern of parts* to match a *feature pattern* in a part. Think of it this way, we make a pattern of bolts to match the pattern of holes in the *'Side Cover'*, this way, *IF* the pattern of holes changes (more or less holes), the pattern of screws in the assembly changes to match it. From the drop down menu in the **"Linear Component Pattern"** select **"Feature Driven Component Pattern"** or the menu **"Insert, Component Pattern, Feature Driven**."

382. - In the "Components to Pattern" selection box select the ¼-20 screw previously made, and in the "Driving Feature" select any of the patterned holes in the '*Side Cover*', except the original hole. When selecting a hole's face, make sure the highlight shows the "*CirPattern1*" name, this way we'll know it's a pattern hole. After selecting the pattern face we can see the preview of screws in each hole and click OK to finish the pattern.

383. - Select the "**Mirror Components**" command either from the menu "Insert, Mirror Components" or the drop-down menu in the "Linear Component Pattern" icon.

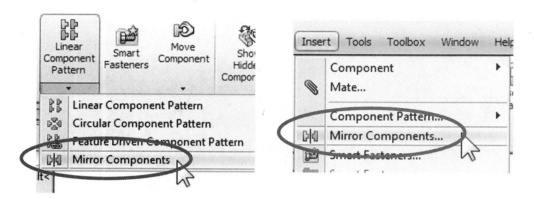

384. – Use the assembly's "*Front Plane*" as the "Mirror Plane" and in the "Components to Mirror:" selection box pick the ¼-20 screw and the "*DerivedCirPattern1*" feature (it will add all the screws in the pattern.) Click in the "Next" arrow to continue to the next step and then OK to finish the mirror.

385. – Save the finished assembly as '*Gear Box Complete*'.

Notes:

Configurations using Design Tables

Previously we covered how to make configurations of parts by manually suppressing features and changing dimensions. While this approach may be adequate when we have 2 or maybe 3 configurations, it gets very complicated to keep track of 5, 10, 20 or more configurations with multiple configured features and dimensions. This is when controlling configurations with a Design Table is a good idea. A Design Table is an Excel file embedded inside the SolidWorks file that controls dimension values, feature suppression states, configuration names, file properties, etc., allowing us to keep track of configurations in a single place.

To use Design Tables either Excel 2007 or 2010 is required. *OpenOffice* spreadsheets are not supported.

386. - For this example, we'll make a simplified version of a screw with only a handful of sizes. Before we make the design table, we need to have a model to configure. Make a new part and add the following sketch in the "*Front Plane*." Remember to add the centerline for the diameter dimensions.

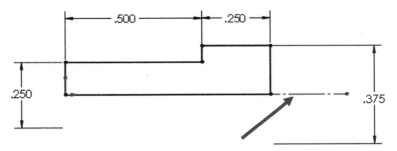

387. - SolidWorks automatically assigns an internal name to all dimensions with the general format *name@feature_name*. We can temporarily see a dimension's name by resting the mouse pointer on top of a dimension, or we can make them always visible (useful when making design tables) using the menu "**View, Dimension Names**."

When adding configurations with different dimension sizes, especially with a design table, it is a good idea to give dimensions a name that allows us to easily identify them. To rename a dimension, select it in the screen and type a new name in its properties. When renaming dimensions, do not worry about the part "*@feature_name*"; SolidWorks will add that automatically when we are finished. Turn on the Dimension Names and rename them as shown.

Another way to change a dimension's name is by double-clicking on a dimension as if to change its value, and typing a name in the top box in the "Modify" dialog box.

388 - After completing the sketch make a revolved boss. After we make a feature, the sketch dimensions are hidden as with every feature we've made before. In order to make model dimensions visible while editing the part, right-mouse-click in the "Annotations" folder in the FeatureManager, and activate the option "Show Feature Dimensions."

389. - Add a hexagonal cut in the head of the screw; make it 0.125″ deep.

390. - Change the cut dimension's names to "*Hex_Drive*" and "*Hex_Depth*." Note that dimensions added in the sketch are shown in black, and dimensions added by the feature are blue.

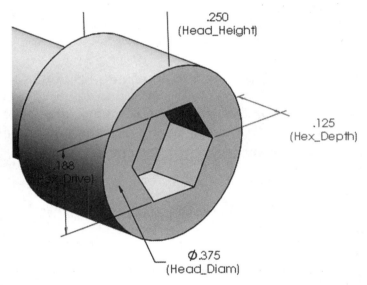

391. - Add a 0.015″ x 45 deg. chamfer to the head and tip of the screw.

392. - After completing the part and renaming the dimensions, we are ready to make the design table. Go to the menu "**Insert, Tables, Design Table**." We'll use the "Auto-create" option that makes adding a design table easier and leave the rest of the options to the default value. When we click on OK, we are presented with a list of all the dimensions in the model; this is where we select the

dimensions that we want to configure. Features and more dimensions can be added to the table later if needed. For this model, select the dimensions indicated. To make multiple selections, hold down the "Ctrl" key while selecting. This is why renaming dimensions is handy, as we know what they are.

393. - After selecting the dimensions to configure, click OK to automatically embed an Excel spreadsheet in the SolidWorks part ready to edit. Since we are using Excel embedded *inside* SolidWorks, our menus and toolbars change to Excel according to Windows' application linking and embedding behavior.

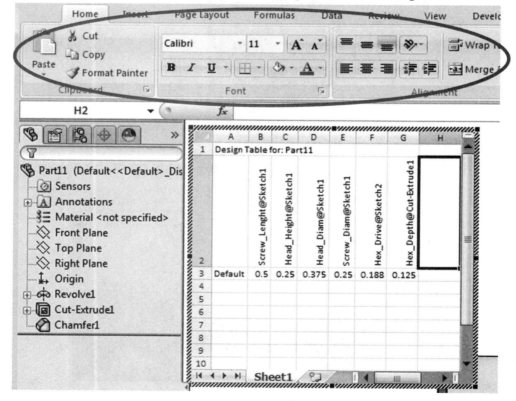

394. - The normal behavior of embedded documents in Windows is to add a thin border around the embedded document. If needed, we can move the Excel file by dragging this border, or resize it from the corners. The borders are very small, be careful not to click outside or you'll exit Excel and go back to SolidWorks.

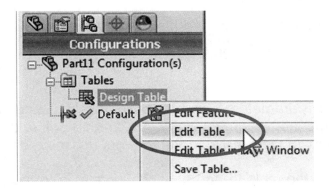

IMPORTANT: If you accidentally click outside the Excel spreadsheet, this is what will happen: you may be told that that a configuration was created, or not, depending on whether the design table was changed or not. To go back to editing the design table, go to the ConfigurationManager, expand the "Tables" folder, make a right-click in the "Design Table" and select "Edit Table." This will get you back to editing the design table embedded in Excel.

395. - Resize the table and columns if needed. As we always have at least one configuration, "Default" is listed in our Design Table with the corresponding values listed under each parameter. Our Design Table now looks like this:

396. - The Design Table holds the information of the parameters that are configured, the configuration names, and values for each parameter in every configuration. The first row holds information about the part. We can type anything we want in this row, as the configuration's data start in the second row.

Configurable parameters are listed in the second row starting at the second column, and configuration names are listed in the first column starting in the third row. Here is a list of the most commonly configured parameters in a part:

Parameter	Format in Design Table	Possible Values
Dimensions (To control dimension value)	*name@feature_name*	Any decimal value
Features (To control if a feature is suppressed or not)	*$STATE@feature_name*	S or *Suppressed* U or *Unsuppressed*
Custom properties (To add custom properties to a configuration)	*$prp@property* *property* is the name of the custom property to add	Any text string

 Many other parameters can be configured including hole wizard sizes, description, center of gravity, tolerances, etc. Look in the SolidWorks help for "Summary of Design Table Parameters" for more details.

397. - Now we'll fill the table to add new configurations to the part. Edit the table and fill it out as shown; note that the "Default" configuration was renamed. The configured dimension were all imported when we created the design table. We don't need to type the dimension names, just the Configuration names and their values (Cells A3 to G8.) Column "F" was formatted to show dimensions as fractions.

	A	B	C	D	E	F	G	H
1	Design Table for: Part11							
2		Screw_Lenght@Sketch1	Head_Height@Sketch1	Head_Diam@Sketch1	Screw_Diam@Sketch1	Hex_Drive@Sketch2	Hex_Depth@Cut-Extrude	
3	6-32×0.5	0.50	0.138	0.226	0.138	7/64	0.064	
4	6-32×0.75	0.75	0.138	0.226	0.138	7/64	0.064	
5	10-32×0.5	0.50	0.19	0.312	0.19	5/32	0.09	
6	10-32×0.75	0.75	0.19	0.312	0.19	5/32	0.09	
7	0.25-20×0.5	0.50	0.25	0.375	0.25	3/16	0.12	
8	0.25-20×0.75	0.75	0.25	0.375	0.25	3/16	0.12	
9								
10								

Sheet1

398. - Now that the Design Table is complete, click anywhere inside the graphics area of SolidWorks to exit the Design Table (and Excel.) We will be told that the configurations have been created. Click OK to continue.

399. - Looking at the ConfigurationManager we see the added configurations. Note that configurations added in the Design Table have an Excel icon. The dimensions configured in the table are now magenta (default setting.) Switch between the configurations to see the different sizes created for each one.

 We can delete the *"Default"* configuration since we are not using it, but we have to change to a different configuration first because we cannot delete the currently active configuration.

400. - To configure additional features we have to edit the Design Table. Right-mouse-click in the "Design Table" and select "**Edit Table**." When asked to add Configurations or Parameters, click "Cancel" to continue.

401. - When the table is presented, the next available cell for adding a new parameter is pre-selected (in our case "H2".) To add the chamfer as a configurable parameter, we can type *$STATE@Chamfer1* directly in the cell, or select the FeatureManager tab to view the features and double-click in the "*Chamfer1*" feature.

Double-click in the "*Chamfer1*" feature will add the correct nomenclature in the table and its current suppression state, in this case *Unsuppressed*. If we leave the value empty, SolidWorks will assume *Unsuppressed*. For short, we can type *S* for *Suppressed* or U for *Unsuppressed*.

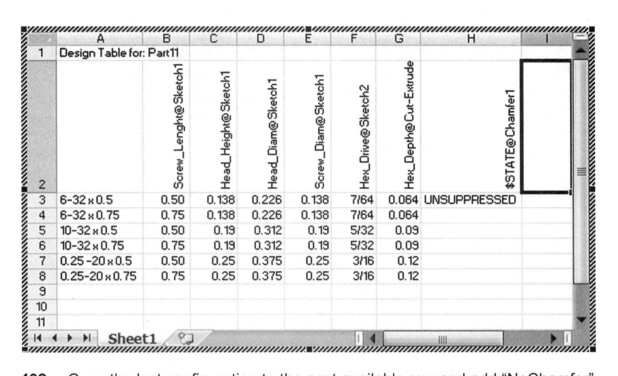

The design table shows:

	A	B	C	D	E	F	G	H	I
1	Design Table for: Part11								
2		Screw_Lenght@Sketch1	Head_Height@Sketch1	Head_Diam@Sketch1	Screw_Diam@Sketch1	Hex_Drive@Sketch2	Hex_Depth@Cut-Extrude	$STATE@Chamfer1	
3	6-32 x 0.5	0.50	0.138	0.226	0.138	7/64	0.064	UNSUPPRESSED	
4	6-32 x 0.75	0.75	0.138	0.226	0.138	7/64	0.064		
5	10-32 x 0.5	0.50	0.19	0.312	0.19	5/32	0.09		
6	10-32 x 0.75	0.75	0.19	0.312	0.19	5/32	0.09		
7	0.25 -20 x 0.5	0.50	0.25	0.375	0.25	3/16	0.12		
8	0.25-20 x 0.75	0.75	0.25	0.375	0.25	3/16	0.12		
9									
10									
11									

Sheet1

402. - Copy the last configuration to the next available row and add "NoChamfer" to the name (SolidWorks does not allow duplicate names for configurations), and suppress "*Chamfer1*" just as an exercise. For short we used ***U*** and ***S*** for suppression states. Feel free to format the Design Table to your liking (it's Excel), as long as you don't change the layout.

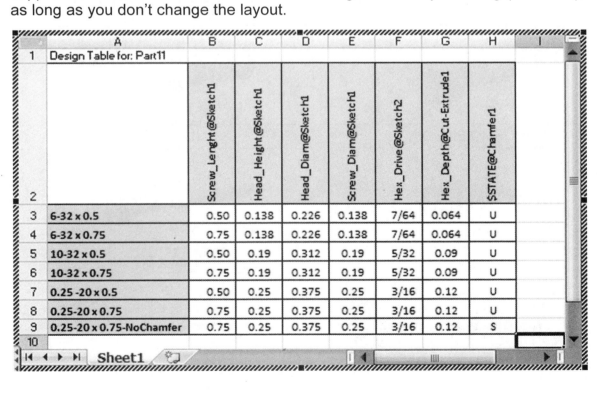

	A	B	C	D	E	F	G	H	I
1	Design Table for: Part11								
2		Screw_Lenght@Sketch1	Head_Height@Sketch1	Head_Diam@Sketch1	Screw_Diam@Sketch1	Hex_Drive@Sketch2	Hex_Depth@Cut-Extrude1	$STATE@Chamfer1	
3	6-32 x 0.5	0.50	0.138	0.226	0.138	7/64	0.064	U	
4	6-32 x 0.75	0.75	0.138	0.226	0.138	7/64	0.064	U	
5	10-32 x 0.5	0.50	0.19	0.312	0.19	5/32	0.09	U	
6	10-32 x 0.75	0.75	0.19	0.312	0.19	5/32	0.09	U	
7	0.25 -20 x 0.5	0.50	0.25	0.375	0.25	3/16	0.12	U	
8	0.25-20 x 0.75	0.75	0.25	0.375	0.25	3/16	0.12	U	
9	0.25-20 x 0.75-NoChamfer	0.75	0.25	0.375	0.25	3/16	0.12	S	
10									

Sheet1

403. - After finishing the changes in the Design Table, return to SolidWorks as we did before, as soon as we leave Excel we get a message letting us know that a new configuration was created. Click OK to acknowledge and continue.

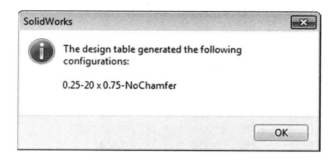

404. - Hide the model dimensions and save the part as "*Screw Design Table*." When adding a configured component to an assembly, it can be configured just like we changed the '*Housing*' from "*Forge"* to "*Machined."* The finished configurations look like this:

0.25 -20 x 0.5	0.25 -20 x 0.75
10-32 x 0.5	10 -32 x 0.75
6-32 x 0.5	6-32 x 0.75
0.25 -20 x 0.75-NoChamfer	

405. - For the screw we just made to be truly useful we have to add it to our own components library, and give it the ability to auto-assemble using SmartMates. First we need to add a new feature called "**Mate Reference**", this feature will tell a part what type of geometry to look for when we add it to an assembly. Select the menu "Insert, Reference Geometry, Mate Reference" or the drop-down menu in the "Reference Geometry" icon.

406. - In the "Primary Reference Entity" select the edge indicated. In the "Mate Reference Type" the only option we can use for a circular edge is "Default" and in "Mate Reference Alignment" leave the option to "Any." Click OK to add the reference. By selecting this edge with these options we will get the "Peg-in-Hole" behavior when we drag-and-drop it from the "Design Library" into an assembly. When adding multiple mate references we can rename them for easier reference.

After the Mate Reference is added we can see it in the FeatureManager, where we can edit or delete it if needed. Save the part to continue.

For simple mates we can use a single mate reference, for more complex mates we can use a second or even a third reference. Mate References can be defined using faces, edges, vertices, axes, planes or the origin. The following table shows the type of entity and mate options available. Using "Default" will try to add the default mate type for the entity in the assembly.

Entity		Mate Reference Types available
Cylindrical Face		• Default • Tangent • Concentric
Round Edge		• Default
Flat Face / Plane		• Default • Tangent • Coincident • Parallel
Axis		• Default • Concentric • Coincident • Parallel
Vertex/Origin		• Default • Coincident

407. – The next step is to add the component to the "Design Library." Open the "Design Library" tab, and press the "Keep Visible" push pin as we need the pane to remain visible for the next step.

408. – Expand the "Design Library" and select the "parts, hardware" folder. To add the screw to the library we can either select the "Add to Library" icon or drag-and-drop the screw from the top of the Feature-Manager either into the lower half of the pane or the folder where we want to save it.

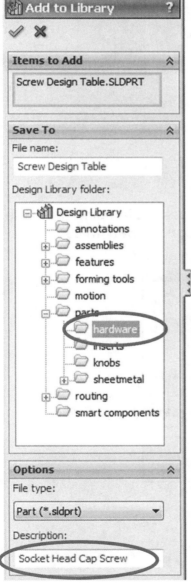

The difference between the two options is that in the "Add to Library" command the screw is pre-selected when we drag and drop it, and using the "Add to Library" icon we have to select the screw in the "Items to Add" selection box.

After selecting (or pre-selecting) the screw, select the folder where we want to store the library and optionally add a description. After pressing OK to add the screw to the hardware folder it is added to the list of available components in the "Design Library." Close the screw file before using it in an assembly, otherwise we'll be asked if we want to use the currently open file.

409. - *Alternate to SolidWorks Toolbox:* Dragging and dropping the screw into an assembly it will have the same behavior as the screw from the Toolbox, the mate reference we added will allow it to automatically add the necessary mates when we drop it in.

After we drop the screw in the hole it will auto assemble using the mate reference and then we'll be able to select the configuration we want to use.

Interference Detection

410. - Go back to the *Gear Box Complete* assembly. One tool that will help us find problems in our assemblies is the "**Interference Detection**" command. We can find it in the "Evaluate" toolbar, or in the menu "**Tools, Interference Detection**." We have designed an interference in the assembly to show the user how to use this tool. Click on "**Interference Detection**" and click on "Calculate." The entire assembly is selected by default.

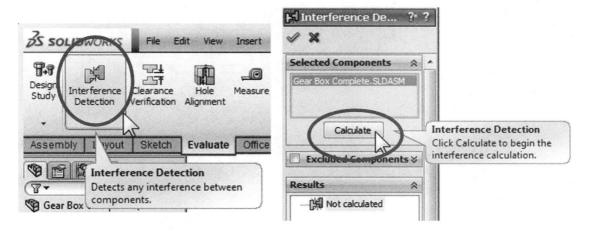

411. - After calculating the interferences, we see many interferences listed in the "Results" window. Most of these are fasteners, because the holes they fit in are smaller than the screw threads. Since we know that, we are going to use an option called "Create fasteners folder." When selected all the fastener interferences will be grouped together, making it easier to identify problem areas that are not fasteners. Turn this option on. The option "Make interfering parts transparent" is on by default, this option will allow us to easily identify the interfering volumes.

NOTE: The fasteners folder option only works with Toolbox generated fasteners.

It's useful to turn on the "Hidden" option in the "Non-interfering Components" box to temporarily hide all the components that are not related to the selected interference, making the problem areas easier to find.

412. – If needed, collapse the "Fasteners" folder and select an interference from the list to see the interfering volumes. Now the designer knows where the problem is, and can take corrective action. In this step ignore the gear-on-gear interference, we'll work on them later. This is a tool that will help us make better designs, but it will only show us where the problems are, and it's up to the designer to fix them.

413. – To avoid checking for and displaying interferences we are not interested in, in this case the gear-on-gear, select each of those interferences and click in the "Ignore" button to hide them. In our example we have three instances, your case may be different depending on the position of each gear. Optionally we can rotate the gears to a position where they do not interfere with each other.

414.- In our case, we know the hole in the '*Housing*' is smaller than the *'Offset Shaft'*, and we need to make the shaft's diameter smaller. To make this change, exit the "Interference Detection" command, and double-click on the shaft's cylindrical surface to reveal the feature's dimensions.

415. - Double-click on the diameter dimension and change its value to 0.575″. Click on the "Rebuild" icon as shown, and then OK to complete the "Modify" command. Rebuilding the model will tell SolidWorks to update any models that were changed, like the *'Offset Shaft'* in this case.

416. - After changing the shaft's diameter run the "**Interference Detection**" command again to confirm that we have resolved the interference between the shaft and the housing, the only interference displayed will be the fasteners.

417. - When we make a change to a part in the assembly, the change is propagated to the part and it's drawing. In our book we have two different versions of the *'Offset Shaft'*, with gear and without. Depending on which version was added to the assembly, that's the one that was changed, and after opening it's drawing the drawing would be up to date as well.

If you have followed the book and added the geared shaft to the assembly, open the 'Offset shaft' part (without the gear) and change its diameter to 0.575". After updating it open the shaft's drawing and verify the shaft's diameter has been updated in the drawing as well. Save and close the drawing file. If asked to save modified files, click on "Save All" to save both the part and the drawing.

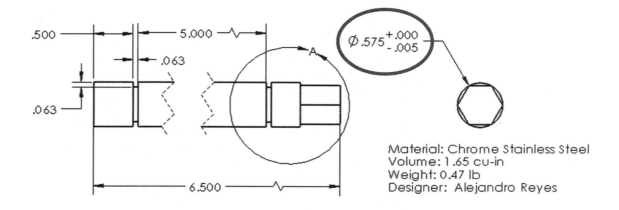

418. - After completing the changes to the offset shaft, we realize that there is another problem with our assembly: The geared shaft cannot be assembled as designed, because it will not fit through the hole in the '*Housing*'. In this case the problem is exaggerated to make it obvious, but most of the time in real life it's not always obvious. To help us find out we can use a tool called "Collision Detection" that allows us to move a part through its range of motion and alert us when it hits another component. To allow the shaft to move freely along its axis we need to suppress the coincident mate added in step 368, we can find it under the "Offset Shaft, Mates" in the FeatureManager.

419. – After suppressing the mate we can click and drag the shaft and it will move and rotate about its axis. To simplify the view, hold down the "Ctrl" key and select the shaft and the housing, make a right-mouse-click and select "Isolate." Every component that is not selected will be hidden from view temporarily and we'll see a new toolbar that will have an "Exit Isolate" button to return to the previous view state. Isolate temporarily hides all the components we are not interested in.

420. – From the Assembly tab select the "Move Component" command. In essence it's the same as dragging a component in the graphics area, but this way we have added options including "Collision Detection" and "Physical Dynamics."

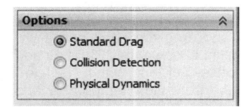

421. – Select "Collision Detection" and activate the "These Components" option. We'll use this option to calculate collisions only between the housing and the shaft, because the more components are included in the analysis the slower the components will move. Select the '*Housing*' and the '*Offset Shaft Gear*' and click on "Resume Drag" to continue the collision detection. Make sure the "Stop at collision", "Highlight faces" and "Sound" options are selected.

Using the "All components" option can be used if our assembly has only a few components and we have a fast computer. The maximum number of components depends on geometry complexity, mates, computer speed, etc.

If we start moving the parts with the "Collision Detection" command and there is an interference between any two components being analyzed, we'll get a warning letting us know about it and the option "Stop on collision" will be disabled. We will continue to get the sound and highlight faces. This is another good reason to limit the number of components included in the analysis.

421. – Click and drag the shaft, notice how the movement is slower than usual and maybe sluggish, depending on the computer's speed. When the helical thread hits the housing's wall, it will highlight the colliding faces and stop.

422. – The collision detection and the interference detection are tools to help us find out if we have design problems that need to be addressed before fabricating the product. After identifying the interference click in "Exit Isolate" to return to the previous view state and Unsuppress the mate that locates the shaft to continue. In the assembly exercises we'll fix the *'Housing'* to allow us to assemble the shaft.

423. – As a final step to finish the assembly we'll add a new type of mate called "Gear." The gear mate allows us to define a rotation ratio between two cylindrical elements, and the two elements don't need to have any type of alignment. In the FeatureManager select the *'Worm Gear Shaft'*, *'Worm Gear Complete'* and *'Offset Shaft Gear'*, and select "Isolate."

424. – Select the "**Mate**" command, expand the "Mechanical Mates" group and select the "Gear Mate." Select the indicated faces and enter 1 for the *'Offset Shaft Gear'* ratio and 22 for the *'Worm Gear Complete'* ratio. Press OK to add the mate and close the mates command.

425. – To test the gear mate click and drag with the left mouse button either shaft to see the effect. Dragging the '*Worm Gear Complete*' will cause the '*Offset Shaft Gear*' to turn fast and vice versa.

 Before adding the "Gear Mate" we can align the gears to a position where there are no interferences between them to make a better looking animation.

426. – Click in the "Exit Isolate" button to return the view to the previous state to finish the assembly. Your assembly '*Gear Box Complete*' is finished and should now look like this.

427. – Instead of hiding a component to view inside of it, we can make it transparent. Select the *'Housing'* in the FeatureManager or the graphics area, and from the pop-up menu select "**Change Transparency**." Turn the gears to see the effect. To make the components opaque again repeat the same process.

428. – An assembly's weight can be calculated the same way as a part using the "**Mass Properties**" command. The difference is that in the assembly, the weight will be the combined weight of the individual components based on the materials they are made of. This is why it's a good idea to always assign a material to each component. Alternatively, mass properties (weight, center of mass and moments of inertia) can be overridden if needed selecting the "**Override Mass Properties…**" button.

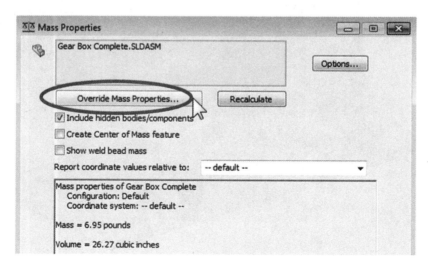

Exploded View

429. - The last step in the assembly will be to make an exploded view for documentation. Exploded views are commonly used to show how the components will be assembled together. Select the "**Exploded View**" icon from the "Assembly" tab or from the menu "**Insert, Exploded View**."

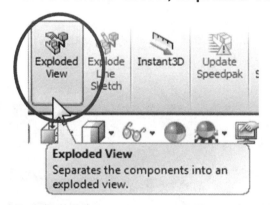

430. - In the Explode PropertyManager we can see the "Settings" selection box is active and ready for us to select the component(s) that will be exploded. For this example, we will leave the option "Auto-space components after drag" off.

431. - To add the first explode step, select the four screws on the *'Top Cover'* and drag the <u>green tip</u> of the manipulator arrow (Y-Direction) upwards as far as you want the screws exploded, or select the direction and enter a distance. Note the ruler as we drag the screws up.

432. - After dragging the arrow, "Explode Step1" is added to the "Explode Steps" list, and the selection box is cleared. Do not click on OK yet; we are going to add more explode steps.

If we need to modify an explode step, select it from the "Explode Steps" list and drag the blue manipulator arrow to the new exploded distance.

433. - For the second explode step, select the *'Top Cover'* and drag the green manipulator arrow up about halfway between the screws and the *'Housing'*.

434. - For the third step, select the six screws on one *'Side Cover'* and drag them to the left using the blue manipulator arrow (Z-Direction.)

435. - The rest of the explode steps are done the same way, selecting the component(s) and dragging the tip of the manipulator arrow along the desired explode direction. The next step is to explode the *'Side Cover'*.

436. - Now explode the *'Worm Gear Shaft'* and the screws from the other side of the gear assembly in one step. Rotate the assembly and select the screws and the shaft, then click-and-drag the manipulator's arrow to explode them.

437. - Now explode the second *'Side Cover'*.

438. - Finally, explode the *'Worm Gear'* and the *'Offset Shaft'* in two different steps to get the exploded view in the next image. Try to group components that will be exploded the same distance and direction at the same time to reduce the number of steps required to document our design. When we finish adding explode steps click OK to finish the **Exploded View** command.

439. - After exploding the assembly, we may want to collapse it. In order to do this, click with the right mouse button at the top of the Feature-Manager in the Assembly name and select "**Collapse**" from the pop-up menu.

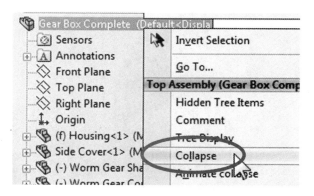

440. - To explode the assembly again, click with the right mouse button at the top of the FeatureManager as we just did, and select "**Explode**." This option will only be available if the assembly has been exploded. In case we need to edit the exploded view steps again, select the "**Exploded View**" icon to bring back the explode PropertyManager.

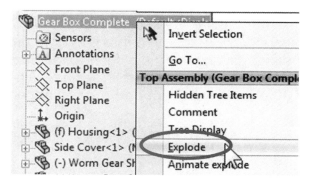

441. - From this same menu we can select "**Animate collapse**" if the assembly is exploded, or "**Animate explode**" if the assembly is collapsed. This brings up the Animation Controller to animate the explosion and optionally record it to video.

Exercises: Modify the 'Housing' to allow the 'Offset Shaft Gear' to be assembled and make the detail drawings for any additional components. Here is a potential solution: Increase the size of the shaft holes in the 'Housing' and add a bushing.

 To create this image the component's display was changed individually using the "Display Pane", here we can hide/show, change display style, change appearance and transparency by component.

Engine Project: Assemble the engine using the parts built in the Part modeling exercises, and make an exploded view. First make the following sub-assemblies as indicated (shown in exploded view) before adding them to the final assembly.

Piston Head Sub Assembly

Internal Retaining Ring

Piston Head

Pin ConRod-Piston

Internal Retaining Ring

Internal Retaining Rings go in the grooves

Connecting Rod Sub Assembly

Connecting Rod Bottom

Connecting Rod

Bushing Top Con Rod

Con Rod Crankshaft Half Bushing

Socket Head Cap Screw 1/4-28 x 5/8"

Crankshaft Sub Assembly

Sequence of components to assemble the engine.

Oil Pan	Crankshaft Sub Assembly	Shaft Seal Gasket	Oil Seal
Oil Pan Gasket	Connecting Rod Sub Assembly	Crank Case Top	Cylinder Gasket
Piston Head Sub Assembly. (Only one Concentric mate to not over define it)	Engine Block	Make the Piston Head **concentric to** the Engine Block	Head Gasket

Cylinder Head	Shaft Seal Cover	Exhaust	Intake

Oil Dip Stick	Socket Head Cap Screws: ¼-20 x ½", ¼-20 x 5/8", 6-32 x ½"		

Washer and Hex Bolt 3/8"-16 x 1-1/4"	Washer, Lock Washer, Hex Bolt 5/16-24 x 1-1/4"

After completing the engine assembly, make a section view as we did in **step 194** and move the crankshaft. If the assembly was made correctly the crankshaft will rotate and the piston will move up and down as it should.

A video of this cross section is available in our website in the downloads section.

After adding all the fasteners the FeatureManager will be *very* long. To make it easier to navigate we can group multiple components together using folders. Select all the fasteners in the FeatureManager, right-mouse-click on them, select "**Add to New Folder**" and rename it "*Fasteners*." This way we can hide, suppress, delete or isolate them all at the same time. Afterwards we can drag-and-drop parts to and from a folder to add or remove items.

As an optional finishing touch before making the exploded view add a spark plug. You can download one from the 3D Content Central website (Free). You have to sign up and log in to access it. The link to the spark plug we used is:

http://www.3dcontentcentral.com/secure/download-model.aspx?catalogid=171&id=86052

Image created using RealView

When making the exploded view we can use the option "Select sub-assembly's parts" to explode sub-assembly components individually, if this option is off the entire sub-assembly will move as a single part.

Extra Credit: Make the assembly of the *Gas Grill* using the parts created in the part modeling Extra Credit project and then add an exploded view for documentation purposes. The grill's cover must be able to open and close. Close the cover using collision detection.

http://mechanicad.com/download.html

Assembly and Design Table Drawings

ITEM NO.	PART NUMBER	DESCRIPTION	QTY.	Material	Weight
1	Housing	CAST P/N 1234-B	1	Cast Alloy Steel	4.38
2	Side Cover	Cast Cover #345	2	AISI 1020	0.36
3	Worm Gear Shaft	Shaft with Hex Drive	1	Chrome Stainless Steel	0.52
4	Worm Gear Complete	Gear P/N ABC-12345	1	Plain Carbon Steel	0.33
5	Offset Shaft Gear	Part No. 1234-ABC	1	Chrome Stainless Steel	0.49
6	Top Cover	Casting #9876	1	Cast Alloy Steel	0.46
7	HX-SHCS 0.138-32x0.5x0.5-S		4		
8	HX-SHCS 0.25-20x0.5x0.5-S		12		

Designer: Alejandro Reyes

TITLE: **Speed Reducer**

SIZE **B** DWG. NO. Gear Box Complete   REV

SCALE: 1:2   WEIGHT: SHEET 1 OF 1

Design Table for: Part1

	Screw_Length@Sketch1	Head_Height@Sketch1	Head_Diam@Sketch1	Screw_Diam@Sketch1	Hex_Drive@Sketch2	Hex_Depth@CUT-Extrude1	S$STATE@Chamfer1
6-32 x 0.5	0.50	0.138	0.226	0.138	7/64	0.064	U
6-32 x 0.75	0.75	0.138	0.226	0.138	7/64	0.064	U
10-32 x 0.5	0.50	0.19	0.312	0.19	5/32	0.09	U
10-32 x 0.75	0.75	0.19	0.312	0.19	5/32	0.09	U
0.25 -20 x 0.5	0.50	0.25	0.375	0.25	3/16	0.12	U
0.25-20 x 0.75	0.75	0.25	0.375	0.25	3/16	0.12	U
0.25-20 x 0.75 -NoChamfer	0.75	0.25	0.375	0.25	3/16	0.12	S

.500 (Screw_Lenght)

.250 (Head_Height)

∅.250 (Screw_Diam)

∅.375 (Head_Diam)

.188 (Hex_Drive)

.015 X 45° (RD1)

UNLESS OTHERWISE SPECIFIED: NAME   DATE

DIMENSIONS ARE IN INCHES
TOLERANCE:
FRACTIONAL±
ANGULAR: MACH± BEND ±
TWO PLACE DECIMAL ±
THREE PLACE DECIMAL ±

DRAWN
CHECKED
ENG APPR.
MFG APPR.
Q.A.
COMMENTS:

Screw Design Table

TITLE:

SIZE **A** DWG. NO. **SHCS**   REV

SCALE: 4:1   WEIGHT: SHEET 1 OF 1

442. - After finishing an assembly it is usually required to make an assembly drawing with a Bill of Materials for assembly instructions and documentation. In this case, we will make a drawing with an exploded view, Bill of Materials (BOM) and identification balloons. To make the drawing, open the assembly *'Gear Box Complete'*. Select the "**Make drawing from part/assembly**" icon as we did with the parts, and make a new drawing using the "B-Landscape" sheet size, with the "Display sheet format" checkbox activated.

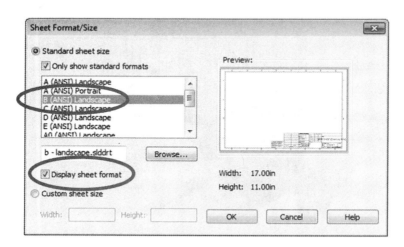

443. - From the "View Palette", drag the "Isometric Exploded" view to the sheet. Change the Display Style to "Shaded with Edges" and change the scale to 1:2 using "Use custom scale" from the "Scale" options box.

When an assembly has an Exploded View, we can change the view to display Exploded or Collapsed after inserting it in the drawing sheet. Right-mouse-click in the assembly view, select "Properties" from the pop-up menu and turn on/off the option "**Show in Exploded State**."

444. - Once we have the exploded isometric view in the drawing, we need to add a **Bill of Materials** (BOM). Select the isometric view from the graphics area by clicking on it, and select the menu "**Insert, Tables, Bill of Materials**", or from the right mouse button menu (in the isometric view), "**Tables, Bill of Materials**."

445. - In this example click OK in the Bill of Materials PropertyManager to accept the default options.

446. - After clicking on OK, we can locate the Bill of Materials in the sheet. Move the mouse and locate the BOM in the top right corner of the drawing. While locating the table, notice the table will snap to the corner. If needed, move the assembly view to make space for the identification balloons that will be added later. The column's width and row's height can be adjusted by dragging the table lines just as with Microsoft Excel. Since we added the "Description" custom property to the *'Worm Gear Shaft'*, *'Worm Gear'* and *'Offset Shaft'*, they are automatically imported into the Bill of Materials.

ITEM NO.	PART NUMBER	DESCRIPTION	QTY.
1	Housing		1
2	Side Cover		2
3	Worm Gear Shaft	Shaft with Hex Drive	1
4	Worm Gear Complete	Gear P/N ABC-12345	1
5	Offset Shaft Gear	Part No. 1234-ABC	1
6	Top Cover		1
7	HX-SHCS 0.138-32x0.5x0.5-S		4
8	HX-SHCS 0.25-20x0.5x0.5-S		12

447. - It is possible to customize the Bill of Materials by adding more columns with information imported from the components' custom properties. To add columns to the table, make a right-mouse-click in the "QTY" cell in the table (or any column you wish), and from the pop-up menu select "**Insert, Column Right**" (or Left...) to locate the new column. For the "Column type" value select "CUSTOM PROPERTY", and from the "Property name" drop down list, select "**Material**." The value will be automatically filled for components with a "Material" custom property.

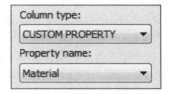

448. - Add another column with the "**Weight**" custom property to complete the table, open all the parts with missing information and add the custom properties needed in the table.

To open a part's file from within the drawing, select the part in the graphics area with the left mouse button and click in the "**Open Part (...)**" icon from the pop-up menu.

Open Part (side cover.sldprt)

449. - To move the table, click-and-drag it from the upper left corner. Column width and row height can be adjusted as needed, and cells, rows, columns or the entire table can be formatted using the pop-up toolbar, just like Microsoft Excel. When finished, your table should look like this.

ITEM NO.	PART NUMBER	DESCRIPTION	QTY.	Material	Weight
1	Housing	CAST P/N 1234-B	1	Cast Alloy Steel	4.38
2	Side Cover	Cast Cover #345	2	AISI 1020	0.36
3	Worm Gear Shaft	Shaft with Hex Drive	1	Chrome Stainless Steel	0.52
4	Worm Gear Complete	Gear P/N ABC-12345	1	Plain Carbon Steel	0.33
5	Offset Shaft Gear	Part No. 1234-ABC	1	Chrome Stainless Steel	0.49
6	Top Cover	Casting #9876	1	Cast Alloy Steel	0.48
7	HX-SHCS 0.138-32x0.5x0.5-S		4		
8	HX-SHCS 0.25-20x0.5x0.5-S		12		

We can add as many custom properties as needed to accurately document our designs and, as we learned, these properties can also be used in the part's detail drawing and the Bill of Materials. Assembly files can also be given custom properties just like individual components.

450. - Now we need to add identification balloons to our assembly drawing to correctly match each item in the assembly view to the item number in the Bill of Materials. Make a right-mouse-click in the assembly drawing view, and from the pop-up menu select "**Annotations, AutoBalloon**" or select the assembly view and go to the menu "**Insert, Annotations, AutoBalloon**."

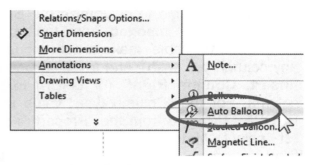

451. - When the AutoBalloon PropertyManager is shown, select the option "Follow Assembly Order" to make the balloons and BOM to follow the component order in the assembly's FeatureManager, in "Balloon Layout" use the "Square" pattern, "Ignore multiple instances" to avoid adding balloons to duplicate components, "Insert magnetic lines" to align the balloons to them, in the "Balloon Settings" options select "Circular", "2 Characters" and "Item Number" to define the size and style of the balloons. If we click-and-drag any of the balloons before we click OK, all the balloons will move in or out at the same time. This can help us locate them closer to the view. When satisfied with the general look of the balloons, click OK to add them to the drawing view. We can modify their positions as needed by dragging them individually later, or dragging the magnetic lines to move all the balloons together.

452. - Click-and-drag the balloons individually to arrange them in the drawing. When dragging a balloon it will snap to the magnetic lines, and magnetic lines can also be moved around the drawing. An arrow's tip can also be dragged to a different area of the part for visibility; if the arrow tip is dragged to a different component, the item number will change to reflect the part that the balloon is attached to. Arrange the balloons as needed to improve readability.

453. - Edit the Sheet Format to add the missing notes in the title block, save the drawing and close the file.

ITEM NO.	PART NUMBER	DESCRIPTION	QTY.	Material	Weight
1	Housing	CAST P/N 1234-B	1	Cast Alloy Steel	4.38
2	Side Cover	Cast Cover #345	2	AISI 1020	0.36
3	Worm Gear Shaft	Shaft with Hex Drive	1	Chrome Stainless Steel	0.52
4	Worm Gear Complete	Gear P/N ABC-12345	1	Plain Carbon Steel	0.33
5	Offset Shaft Gear	Part No. 1234-ABC	1	Chrome Stainless Steel	0.49
6	Top Cover	Casting #9876	1	Cast Alloy Steel	0.48
7	HX-SHCS 0.138-32x0.5x0.5-S		4		
8	HX-SHCS 0.25-20x0.5x0.5-S		12		

Designer: Alejandro Reyes

TITLE:
Speed Reducer

Gear Box Complete

433

454 . – A drawing of a part with a design table is essentially the same as any other drawing, with the only difference that we can add the Design Table to the drawing. Make a new drawing using the '*Screw Design Table*' part, Right-mouse-click in a part's view and select "**Tables, Design Table**" from the pop-up menu. In the drawing we can turn on the dimension names to help identify the dimensions using the menu "**View, Dimension Names**."

Design Table for: Part11	Screw_Lenght@Sketch1	Head_Height@Sketch1	Head_Diam@Sketch1	Screw_Diam@Sketch1	Hex_Drive@Sketch2	Hex_Depth@Cut-Extruded	SSTATE@Chamfer1
6-32 x 0.5	0.50	0.138	0.226	0.138	7/64	0.064	U
6-32 x 0.75	0.75	0.138	0.226	0.138	7/64	0.064	U
10-32 x 0.5	0.50	0.19	0.312	0.19	5/32	0.09	U
10-32 x 0.75	0.75	0.19	0.312	0.19	5/32	0.09	U
0.25 -20 x 0.5	0.50	0.25	0.375	0.25	3/16	0.12	U
0.25-20 x 0.75	0.75	0.25	0.375	0.25	3/16	0.12	U
0.25-20 x 0.75-NoChamfer	0.75	0.25	0.375	0.25	3/16	0.12	S

 When we add a design table to a drawing, we will get a snapshot of the Excel table as it was last used in the part. To modify the design table we have to go back to the part and edit the design table.

Engine Project: Make an assembly drawing of each sub-assembly and one of the exploded Engine Assembly Use the following images as a guide.

For the "Connecting Rod Sub Assembly" use the "A-Portrait" template, for the "Engine Assembly" drawing use the "C-Landscape" template to better accommodate the larger component. Feel free to format the BOM to your liking.

ITEM NO.	PART NUMBER	DESCRIPTION	QTY.
1	Connecting Rod		1
2	Connecting Rod bottom		1
3	Con Rod Crankshaft Half Bushing		2
4	Bushing Top Con Rod		1
5	HX-SHCS 0.25-28x0.625x0.625-S		2

Connecting Rod Sub Assembly

ITEM NO.	PART NUMBER	DESCRIPTION	QTY.
1	Crankshaft		1
2	Sealed Needle Bearing		2
3	Retaining Ring Crankshaft Bearing		2

Crankshaft Sub Assy

ITEM NO.	PART NUMBER	DESCRIPTION	QTY.
1	Piston Head		1
2	Pin ConRod-Piston		1
3	Internal Retaining Ring		2

Piston Head Sub Assy

ITEM NO.	PART NUMBER	DESCRIPTION	QTY.
1		Oil Pan	1
2		Crankshaft Sub Assy	1
3		Shaft Seal Gasket	1
4		Oil Seal	1
5		Oil Pan Gasket	1
6		Connecting Rod Sub Assembly	1
7		Crank Case Top	1
8		Cylinder Gasket	1
9		Piston Head Sub Assy	1
10		Engine Block	1
11		Head Gasket	1
12		Cylinder Head	1
13		Shaft Seal Cover	1
14		Exhaust	1
15		Intake	1
16		Oil Dip Stick	1
17	HX-SHCS 0.25-28x0.625x0.625-S		12
18	HX-SHCS 0.25-28x0.5x0.5-S		6
19	HX-SHCS 0.138-32x0.5x0.5-S		4
20	Preferred Narrow FW 0.3125		4
21	Preferred Narrow FW 0.3125		4
22	HBOLT 0.3125-18x1.25x0.75-N		4
23	HBOLT 0.3125-18x1.25x0.875-S		4
24	Regular LW 0.3125		4
25		Spark Plug	1

DETAIL A
SCALE 2 : 1

Engine Assembly

Analysis: SimulationXpress

Study name: SimulationXpress Study
Plot type: Static nodal stress Stress
Deformation scale: 15.9445

Max: 25,327.7

Min: 38.4

von Mises (psi)

25,327.7
23,220.3
21,112.8
19,005.4
16,897.9
14,790.5
12,683.1
10,575.6
8,468.2
6,360.7
4,253.3
2,145.8
38.4

Yield strength: 39,885.4

Notes:

Background. Why Analysis?

Simulation is a very important tool in engineering. Computers and software have come a long way since the early analysis tools first became available, and modern tools have made simulation a lot easier to use, faster, more accurate and more accessible than ever, enabling designers and engineers to check their design, make sure it's safe, understand how it will deform, if it will fail and under what circumstances, or how it will perform in any given environment (temperature, pressure, vibrations, etc.)

The biggest advantage, by far, when analyzing a design is that we will have a safe design, and at the same time, save money by making decisions as to what materials to use, component sizes, features and even appearance early in the design process, when it is still all in *"paper"* (maybe a more appropriate term now would be *'Bites'* ☺) and cheaper to modify. As the product development process advances beyond the design stage, making design changes to a product is increasingly more expensive as we approach the manufacturing stage.

Picture it this way: Imagine we design a new cellular phone that looks really nice. We make molds, tooling, order parts, and set up an assembly line. Soon the phones start selling, and a month later, we start getting customer complaints: when the call button is pressed hard, the battery cover falls off. Then, *after* we know we have a problem, we run an analysis and find out that *we should have* had a thicker *this or that*, with a *widget* in between the *thingamajig* and the *thingamabob*, and those changes would solve the problem. Now, all we need to do is to change the design, the tooling, the assembly line, marketing, and above all, convince every customer that it is fixed. At this point, our customers' perception of our company and credibility are destroyed. This is usually the most expensive result. It's easy to see why making analysis of our products early in the process will help us design better products and save money and resources.

With that said, it also has to be noted that the simple fact of making a simulation does not guarantee that our designs will be successful, as there are many factors involved. Reasons for product failure include using the product beyond its designed capacity, abuse, material imperfections, fabrication processes and things and circumstances we could have never thought of. This is where the designer needs to take into account every possible scenario, and of course, simulate it as realistically as possible with the correct analysis tools.

SolidWorks includes a *basic analysis package* called "**SimulationXpress**." As its name implies, it has limited functionality that allows only certain scenarios to be analyzed. In order to understand what these limitations are, first we need to learn a little about how analysis works. A general overview of the inner workings of analysis is as follows:

Analysis, also known as "Finite Element Analysis", is a mathematical method where we divide a component's geometry into hundreds or thousands of small pieces (*elements*), where they are all connected to one or more

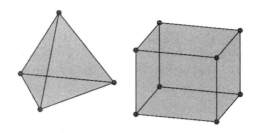

neighboring elements by the vertices (called *nodes* in analysis.) The elements have simple geometry that can be easily analyzed using stress analysis formulas. Elements are usually tetrahedral or hexahedral for most solid models. There are other types of elements including shell and linear elements. SimulationXpress uses tetrahedral elements.

In order for us to make a simulation, we need to know what the component is made of (physical properties of the material), how it is supported (Restraints), and what forces are acting on it (Loads). The next step is to break down the model into small elements; this process is called meshing. The result is called the **mesh**; in SimulationXpress the only input we give, if we choose to, is to define the average element size. SimulationXpress automatically creates the mesh for us.

The next step is to define how the component is supported; in other words, which faces, edges or vertices are restrained. Each node has six degrees of freedom, meaning that each node can move along X, Y and Z and rotate about the X, Y and Z axes. Restraints limit the degrees of freedom (DOF) of the nodes in the face or edge that they are applied to. SimulationXpress limits the user to restraining (Fix) all DOF in faces. In other words, they are completely immovable.

This approach is sufficient for simple analyses, but in order to obtain more accurate solutions, a more realistic simulation must be used that allows selective displacement and rotation of element nodes.

Now that we know how the model is supported, we need to define the Loads (forces) that act upon it. SimulationXpress only allows Forces and Pressures to be applied to model faces. We can define the Loads to be normal to the face they are applied to or perpendicular to a reference plane.

Another limitation of SimulationXpress is it can only make **Linear Static Stress Analysis**. Stress is defined as the internal resistance of a body when it is deformed and is measured in units of Force divided by Area. For example, if we load a bar with a 1 in^2 cross section area with a 1 Lb load, we'll have a stress of 1 Lb/in^2. The stress depends on the forces and the geometry regardless of the material used. The material properties will make a difference as the model will deform more or less.

The "Static" part means the model is immovable; in other words, the restraints will not let the model move with the applied loads. Loads and restraints are in equilibrium, otherwise the analysis would be "Dynamic."

The "Linear" part implies the deformation of the model is proportional to the forces applied; twice the force, twice the deformation. Deformations are generally small compared to the overall size of the part and occur in the **Elastic** region of the "Stress-Strain" curve of the material used. If we remove the force, the model returns to its original shape like a spring; if we apply a force, the part will deform, twice the force, twice the deformation. If we remove the force, the part returns to the original size.

In general terms, the **Yield Stress** is the point where the stress-strain curve is no longer linear. If a material is stressed beyond the Yield Stress it will be permanently deformed. In this case we will have **Plastic Deformation**. Thinking of the spring before, if we pull the spring too far, it is permanently deformed, meaning it had plastic deformation. Once the yield stress is exceeded, the analysis results of Simulation-Xpress are invalid. In this case we need to change our design, geometry, loads or material so that the maximum stress in the model never exceeds the material's yield stress.

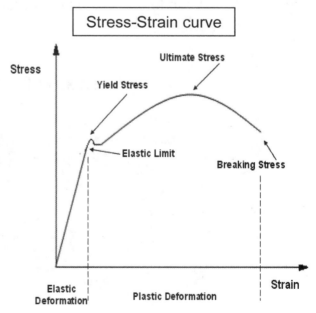

Analysis of a simple part

455. - To show the SimulationXpress functionality, make the following part to make an analysis. Assign the material "Aluminum 6061-T6." *Tip: Make the part with square ends and round them using a "Full Round Fillet."*

456. - We will add forces in the bottom holes perpendicular to the model and support it from the top hole.

457. - In order to better simulate the force, we need to divide the bottom cylindrical faces in two parts, as the force applied will only be acting in one half of the cylindrical face. To accomplish this, we will use the "**Split Line**" command. The first thing we need to do to split the faces in two is to make a sketch in one side of the model (left or right) as indicated. The sketch is a single line.

 Using the "Split Face" command is a common practice in analysis to simulate applying a load in an region of a component's face.

458. - While still in the sketch, select "**Curves, Split Line**" from the Features tab. In "Type of Split" select the "Projection" option; this means that the current sketch will be projected over the faces to split. "Current Sketch" will be pre-selected. Select both of the cylindrical faces to split and click OK to continue. Notice the bottom faces are now divided (split) into two.

459. - Now that we have prepared our model for analysis, activate the SimulationXpress wizard using the menu "**Tools, SimulationXpress**" or in the Evaluate tab in the CommandManager.

460. - The SimulationXpress wizard is integrated in the Task Pane and is automatically displayed. Select "Options", set units to English, turn the checkbox to display annotations for minimum and maximum in the results plot to ON, and leave the results location to the default 'temp' folder. Click "Next" to continue.

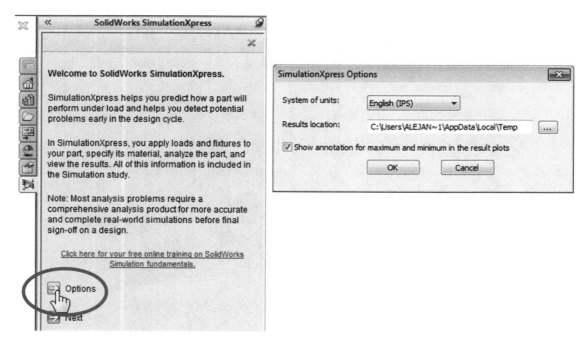

461. - The first step will be to define the "Fixtures", referring to the faces that will be completely rigid (all six degrees of freedom restrained.) We are also given a warning letting us know that the results in the regions close to the fixtures may be unrealistic, and more accurate results can be achieved with *SolidWorks Simulation Professional* by simulating a more realistic restraint condition. Select "Add a Fixture" to define how the part will be supported. We are now presented with the Fixture selection box; select the cylindrical face at the top and click OK to finish. For this example we only need one fixture.

462. - If more Fixtures were needed, select "Add a Fixture" as needed until all the necessary restraints are in place. The SimulationXpress Study now shows the "Fixed-1" condition and "Fixtures" shows a green checkmark letting us know this step is complete. Click Next to continue.

463. - We are now in the "Loads" section of the analysis, and ready to apply the external forces or pressures that will act on the part. The forces that we are adding will be 250 lbf in each face (total of 500 lbf) perpendicular to the part's "*Front Plane*" in each of the two bottom holes.

Select "**Add a Force**" to show the "Force" dialog box. Here we'll select one side of each of the two faces we split earlier; make the force value 250 lbf. To make the forces perpendicular to the part, select the option "Selected Direction" and from the fly-out FeatureManager, select the "*Front Plane*."

 If we don't give the force a direction, it will be normal to the selected faces, making the force radial to the cylindrical surface.

Make sure the option "Per Item" is selected, as we want to apply 250 lbf to each face; if the "Total" option is selected, the 250 lbf force would be equally distributed over the faces selected. In our example the direction of the force doesn't make any difference since our part is symmetrical, but be aware that, if needed, we can change the direction of the force using the "Reverse Direction" box.

Click OK when done and select "Next" from the SimulationXpress wizard at the right to continue. If we need to add more forces or pressures to our analysis click on "Add a Force" or "Add a Pressure" as required.

464. - The "Force-1" condition is added to the SimulationXpress Study and we can see the preview of the forces applied to the faces and their direction. Now "Loads" shows a green checkmark letting us know this step is complete. If we need to add more forces or pressures to other model faces, or modify this one, we would do it in this step. Click Next to continue.

465. - The next step is to define the material that will be used for the part. This is important, because as we explained earlier, we need to know the physical properties of the material being analyzed. Since we had previously assigned a material to the part before starting the analysis (Aluminum 6061-T6), this step is already marked as complete. We can see the green checkbox next to "Material" in the SimulationXpress wizard as well as the Young's Modulus and Yield Strength values for reference. If we not defined a material before starting the analysis, we can select "Change Material" and pick one from the materials list. Click "Next" to continue.

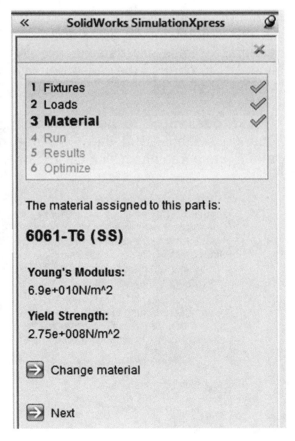

466. - Now that we have given SimulationXpress the minimum information to make an analysis (Fixtures, Forces and Material), we are ready to make the mesh (break the model into smaller 'finite' elements) and run our simulation.

467. - At this point we have an option to run the analysis with the default settings for the mesh or change them. In general, using a smaller mesh size generates more elements that lead to a more accurate solution, however, increasing the number of elements also increases the time and computing resources needed to run the simulation. As a general rule, if our maximum stresses are close to the acceptable limits, try using a slightly smaller mesh element. SimulationXpress allows us to change the mesh density, or the general size of the elements, under "Mesh Parameters."

If desired or needed, the mesh parameters can be modified by selecting "Change settings" and then "Change mesh density." In our example we'll use default mesh settings. Click OK to continue.

ABOUT REDUCING MESH SIZE: Making the mesh size smaller improves results accuracy up to a certain degree, and it comes a point where reducing the element's size does not significantly improve accuracy in sequential solutions; this is called convergence, and is measured in percentage of change from one solution to the next. For example, if the highest stress value is within a certain percentage of the previous study, we can say that we have reached convergence and call our results valid.

In order to start considering reducing the mesh size and look for convergence, our results MUST be below the yield stress and preferably have no stress concentrations in our analysis. After those conditions have been met, we can start to re-run the analysis reducing the mesh size a little at a time (10% reduction is a good starting point.) Convergence values depend on the accuracy needed and can vary around 2% to 5% or even higher. If these values seem high and/or your design has a factor of safety under 10% you may want to consider analyzing your design with a dedicated analysis package to simulate real world situations and improve the accuracy of your analysis in order to be safe.

468. - As soon as we click OK in the "Mesh" dialog box, the model is meshed, in other words, breaking the model into many small pieces (*Finite Elements*.) Then we can see the meshed model ready for analysis.

469. - Now that the model is meshed, select **"Run Simulation"** from the SimulationXpress wizard. What happens next, in the simplest terms, is that the solver (the part that actually calculates stresses and displacements) will generate an equation for each element, with an unknown variable at each node. Since adjacent elements share nodes between them this generates a very large matrix of hundreds or thousands of simultaneous equations. The solver makes the equations, solves the unknown variables at every node and the result for each node is the node's displacement or deformation. Based on the physical properties of the material, we can calculate the stresses in the model at each node.

Since this is a small model it only takes a second to finish the analysis.

470. - When the solver is finished, we see an animation of the deformed model.

471. - The model deforms as we expected in the direction of the force, so we can proceed to view the results. If the model had not deformed as expected, we would have to go back to modify the fixtures and loads to make the necessary corrections. Select "**Yes, continue**" to view the analysis results.

Click in "Show Von Misses Stress" to view the resulting stresses calculated using the **von Mises** method, which is the most commonly used criteria for isotropic materials (materials with the same physical properties in all directions), mostly metals. The deformation is exaggerated for visual clarity (in this case 7.5 times.)

It is important to know that, by the very nature of the Finite Element Analysis process, the results are an *approximation* to the actual physical phenomenon, and solving such a large number of simultaneous equations will most likely return slightly different values for stress and displacement results. However, the resulting values should be, in general, very close to the results shown in this book, assuming that the analysis is defined the same way (geometry, material, loads and restraints) and the mesh size is the same. The accuracy of any analysis will depend on how well the geometry is modeled, as well as how closely material properties, loading and restraining conditions match the actual physical conditions and mesh size. An analysis done with SimulationXpress should only be considered as a general guide and never a substitute for a complete and properly modeled analysis using accurate loading and restraining conditions.

472. - In these results, we can see the Maximum Stress in the model is approximately 38,000 psi, very close to the Yield Strength of 39,885 psi. Based on these results, the lowest Factor of Safety in our model is approximately 1.05. The color-coded stress scale will help in finding the stresses in the rest of the model.

The Factor of Safety is calculated by dividing the material's yield strength by the maximum stress in the model. We are interested in finding the lowest value because if any area of the model has a factor of safety below 1, this means the stress is higher than the material's Yield Strength; our model will have permanent deformation and will be therefore considered to have failed.

 Note that we are talking about permanent deformation and not breaking. To yield does not necessarily mean that it will break; it will break if we reach the Breaking Stress. For many analyses, a permanent deformation is almost always considered to fail.

The different values for **Factor of Safety** (FOS) mean:

Value	Meaning
> 1	The stress at this location in the part is less than the yield strength and is safe. Depending on the specific application, we may have to design with a higher FOS to ensure our design is safe and have room for unexpected loads.
= 1	The stress at this location in the part is exactly the yield strength. This part has started or is about to yield (deform plastically) and will most likely fail if the forces acting on the model are slightly more than the forces used in the analysis.
< 1	The stress at this location in the part has exceeded the yield strength of the material and the component will fail with the analysis parameters used, either deforming plastically or breaking.

473. - To see how safe our design is, type 2 in the Factor of Safety box and click "Show where factor of safety (FOS) is below." Areas under the specified factor of safety (*unsafe*) are shown in red, and the areas over the factor of safety (*safe*) are shown blue. Essentially, using a FOS=2, every area colored in red will fail.

474. - Now activate "**Show Displacement**"; this way we can see how much our model deforms under the current conditions. The maximum deformation is 0.1″ at the bottom of the part, as expected since the top is rigidly supported. (The values in the scale are listed using scientific notation.)

475. - Select "Done viewing results" to move to the next screen where we can generate reports either in Word or eDrawings format. Selecting "Generate report" will generate the files needed for the report and will allow us to fill in additional information before creating it. It will include information as well as screen captures of results and details of the analysis including loads, fixtures and material properties.

476. - Selecting "Generate eDrawings file" will make an eDrawings file with the analysis results. The main difference from the Microsoft Word report is that, in eDrawings, we can rotate the models, turn the mesh on or off, zoom in or out and easily share the results with other people.

477. - What we are going to do now is to change a dimension in the model and re-run the analysis to see how much the results change. Click to close the SimulationXpress wizard. When asked if we want to save the results select "Yes" from the dialog box.

478. – For this example change the 0.875″ thickness dimension to 1.125″ and rebuild the model.

479. - After rebuilding the model, select the SimulationXpress wizard icon to go back to the analysis. Notice the warning icon in the Simulation-Xpress study. This warning icon indicates that we have a problem; in this case the results are no longer valid because we changed the model, and since the geometry is different the mesh is different and therefore the results are invalid, they are outdated.

480. - Since we only changed the geometry and no other loading or restraining conditions, to update the results, all we need to do is to make a right-mouse-click at the top of the analysis tree and select "**Run**" from the pop-up menu to update the results. SimulationXpress will automatically re-mesh the model to account for the geometric changes, and run the analysis.

481. - After running the analysis with the updated geometry, we see the updated results. Now we have a maximum von Mises stress of 25,324 psi, giving us a minimum factor of safety of 1.57 and a maximum displacement of 0.05". Depending on the intent of our design, and industry accepted practices, this may, or may not be sufficient to consider our design safe.

Model name: Analysis part
Study name: SimulationXpress Study
Plot type: Static displacement Displacement
Deformation scale: 15.9445

URES (in)

5.017e-002
4.599e-002
4.181e-002
3.763e-002
3.345e-002
2.927e-002
2.509e-002
2.091e-002
1.672e-002
1.254e-002
8.362e-003
4.181e-003
3.937e-032

Min: 3.937e-032

Max: 5.017e-002

SolidWorks SimulationXpress

1 Fixtures
2 Loads
3 Material
4 Run
5 **Results**
6 Optimize

Results

Show von Mises stress

Show displacement

Show where factor of safety (FOS) is below: 1

Based on the specified parameters, the lowest factor of safety(FOS) found in your design is 1.57477

Use these controls to view the animation.

Play animation

Stop animation

Done viewing results

CHALLENGE: SimulationXpress includes an Optimization wizard that can be accessed after reviewing the results and reports; select "Done viewing results" and click on "Next" to continue to the optimization wizard and select "Yes" when asked to optimize your model.

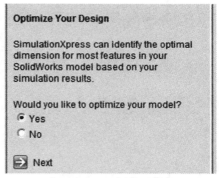

Optimize Your Design

SimulationXpress can identify the optimal dimension for most features in your SolidWorks model based on your simulation results.

Would you like to optimize your model?
◉ Yes
○ No

Next

The Optimization wizard helps us find the lightest model (minimum mass) that complies with the constraints defined. SimulationXpress allows only one dimension to be varied within a range of values defined by the user; the constraints of the optimization can be a minimum factor of safety, a maximum von Mises stress or a maximum displacement.

Run the optimization analysis and try to find a better solution that meets a minimum factor of safety of 1.5 by varying the part's thickness. To run the optimization we have to define a range of values for the dimension, in our case we'll vary the dimension between 0.875" and 1.5". The optimization wizard will calculate five values for the dimension between the range of values, run the analysis for each one and determine the optimum value.

Note: In order for optimization to work, we need to have a study with a factor of safety higher than what we need, basically *over designed*. If the study has a high factor of safety, we can optimize the model to make the part lighter, and still have a factor of safety that meets our design requirements.

A final word on analysis

The analysis world is a very fascinating one that gives us highly sophisticated and powerful tools to predict how machines, products or designs will perform in any given scenario, and allows us to anticipate the best way to assure their safe operation. However, it is extremely important to make sure the correct assumptions for restraints, loads and external conditions are applied to a model in order to correctly simulate the actual physical phenomena, as the accuracy and reliability of the results are directly tied to them. Talking about results, it's just as important to understand what the results obtained from an analysis mean in order to correctly interpret them and avoid over designing, or putting our designs at risk for failure.

As we explained before, SimulationXpress is a *first-pass-analysis* tool. This means that its purpose is to give us a general idea of how the design will perform within the set of applied conditions. If our design is not *comfortably* safe, and/or we know this is a critical component of the design, it may be better to perform a more complete analysis using the full suite of SolidWorks Simulation software, where we can add more realistic loading, restraining and external conditions. Besides, SimulationXpress is only capable of performing linear static analysis; therefore, if we anticipate that a model will be exposed to temperature, vibrations, large deformations, uses non-linear materials, or other conditions that cannot be correctly modeled with SimulationXpress, those analyses should be done using a version of SolidWorks Simulation (or any other analysis software package) capable of properly modeling those situations.

Analysis and simulation can be a very complex subject depending on the task being analyzed, and depending on the specifics of it, a higher understanding of mechanics of materials, physics, vibrations, heat transfer and many other areas will be likely needed in order to properly setup, analyze and interpret the results. An analysis can be as simple as a linear stress analysis in a small part like our example, or as complex as a space ship re-entering the atmosphere taking into account forces, temperatures, vibrations, pressure, radiation, phase changes, aerodynamics, etc., and based on our analysis and results, astronauts would be returning home safely, or not.

Ultimately, safety is the main reason why we make analysis, and why it has to be done right, with the right set of tools and more importantly, the right knowledge.

Exercise: Make a copy of the *'Crankshaft'* part and rename it *'Crankshaft Analysis'*. Add a split line to divide the face indicated and run an analysis using SimulationXpress using the information given for forces and restraints.

1200 Lbf

RESTRAINT TO SIMULATE BEARINGS

Collaboration: eDrawings

How to collaborate with non-SolidWorks users

Sometimes we need to collaborate with other members of the design team in the same room, same building, or even across the world. With the convenience of e-mail, it's easier than ever to share our designs using eDrawings. We can send our extended design team, customers or suppliers a file by e-mail with all the design information needed for them to review and send back feedback to the designer. A big advantage of eDrawings is that it is available for both Windows and Macintosh computers, and recently for iPad and iPhone.

We can generate eDrawings files from Parts, Assemblies, Drawings and simulation studies. The only thing we need to do is to press the Publish eDrawings File icon from the "Save" fly-out toolbar, or go to the menu "**File, Publish to eDrawings**" while the document we want to share is active. The eDrawings viewer will be loaded with the same document. After we generate an eDrawings file, it becomes a *read only* file; we cannot modify it, but we can print it, zoom in or out, section it, etc. For this example, we'll publish an eDrawings file from the '*Gear Box*' assembly drawing. Depending on your installation of eDrawings, your screen will look something like this:

If the eDrawings file is generated using SolidWorks Office Professional or the educational edition, the eDrawings Professional version is loaded. eDrawings Professional includes additional options, including tools to move the components in assemblies, measure, add markups and stamps and, if it's a part or assembly, make section views of the models.

The Previous, Stop, Next and Play buttons will allow you to navigate different views if you have a multiple view drawing, or to go from one view orientation to the next in Parts and Assemblies. Pressing the "Play" icon will animate the views, and will change from one to the next. At any time, the animation can be stopped, and the view zoomed in, rotated and panned.

	While in an eDrawings of an assembly, the parts can be moved by dragging them. To return them to their original location, double-click on them or click in the Home icon.
	If the assembly has an exploded view, in the "Explode View" tab we can explode or collapse the assembly and animate as well.
	Part and assembly eDrawings can be sectioned. Select the "Section" icon, and pick a plane to section about from the options. To move the section plane, simply drag it in the graphics area.
	Part, assembly and drawing eDrawings can be measured. To help protect confidential data, this option is disabled at the time of saving and can be enabled per document.

To activate the "Enable measure" option when saving a published eDrawings file, we have to create an eDrawings file using the menu "**File, Save As...**" and from the "Save as type" selection list pick "eDrawings", press the "Options" button and activate the "Okay to measure this eDrawings file" checkbox. Otherwise every eDrawings file we publish will have the measure tool disabled.

☑ Okay to measure this eDrawings file

By enabling this option, a recipient of this document can measure the geometry in the eDrawings Viewer.

The most powerful option in eDrawings Professional is the markup tools to allow anyone to add annotations to a file, and send it back to the generator to make the required modifications.

The markup tools allow us to add:

- Dimensions
- Notes
- Images
- Clouds with text
- Lines
- Rectangles
- Circles
- Arcs and
- Splines, etc.
-

After creating the eDrawings file, we have to save it. eDrawings allows us to save the files in different ways.

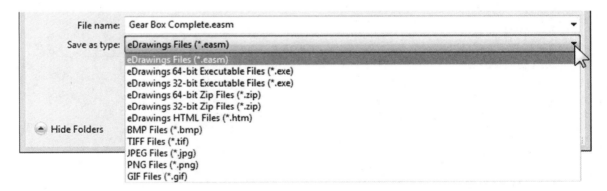

Saving as an eDrawings File (*.edrw) will result in a very small file size that can be easily emailed. The only thing the recipient needs to do is to install the free eDrawings viewer in their computer.

Saving as an HTML file (*.html) will create a web page that can be e-mailed. eDrawings will be loaded automatically if it is already installed in the computer; if it is not installed, the web browser will ask to install and run the corresponding plug-in. Optionally, a link to download the eDrawings viewer is listed at the bottom of the web page.

Notes:

Final Comments

By completing the exercises in this book, we learned how to apply many different SolidWorks features and the various options to common design tasks. As we stated at the beginning, this book is meant to be an introduction to SolidWorks, and as the reader was able to see, the breadth of options and possibilities available to the user after completing this book are enough to accomplish many different tasks from part and assembly modeling to detailing in a short time, using the most commonly used commands, including making a stress analysis with the included SimulationXpress software.

We hope this book serves as a stepping stone for the reader to learn more. A curious reader will be able to venture into more advanced features, and take advantage of the similarities and consistency of the user interface to his/her advantage. We tried very hard to make the content as understandable and easy to follow as possible, as well as to get the reader working on SolidWorks almost immediately, maximizing the "hands-on" time.

After completing all parts, drawings, an assembly including the fasteners, exploded view and the assembly drawing complete with a Bill of Materials, the reader is ready to apply the learned concepts in different design projects.

As a follow-up, be sure to continue learning SolidWorks with the *Level II* book; go further and learn about Sheet Metal, Surfacing, Mold Making and more.

One final tip: If you get lost, or can't find what you are looking for while working in SolidWorks, click with the right mouse button. Chances are, what you are looking for is in that pop-up menu. ☺

Notes:

Appendix

Document templates

One of the main reasons to have multiple templates is to have different settings, especially units. We can have millimeter and inch templates, pre-defined materials for part templates, dimensioning standards, etc. and every time we make a new part based on that template, the new document will have the same settings of the template. A good idea is to have a folder to store our templates, and add it to the list of SolidWorks templates.

Using *Windows Explorer*, make a new folder to store our new templates. For this example we'll make a new folder in the Desktop called *"MySWTemplates*." In SolidWorks, go to the menu **"Tools, Options, System Options, File Locations**." From the drop down menu select "Document Templates."

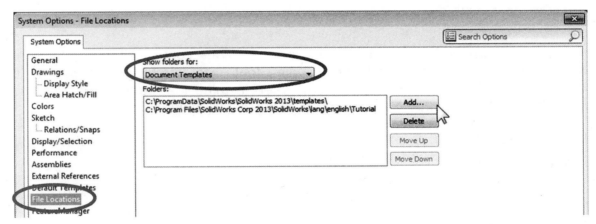

Click the "Add" button and locate the folder we just made to save the templates. Click OK when done. You will now see the additional template folder listed.

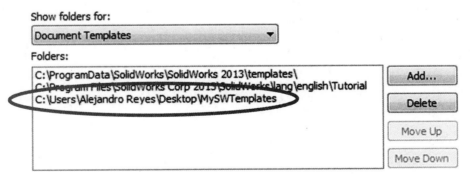

To create a new template, make a new Part, Assembly or Drawing file, and go to the menu "**Tools, Options, Document Properties.**" Everything we change in this tab is saved with the template. The most common options changed in a template are Units, Sketch Grid, Detailing Standards and Annotation Fonts. Let's review them in the order that they appear in the options.

The first section is "Drafting Standard"; here we can change the dimensioning standard to ANSI, ISO, DIN, JIS, etc.; by changing the standard, all the necessary changes will be made to arrows, dimensions, annotations, etc., according to the selected standard.

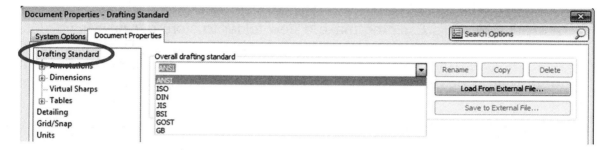

The "**Annotations**" and "**Dimensions**" sections contain all the options for annotation and dimension settings including font, size, arrow type, appearance and every configurable option for them. Keep in mind that setting the "Drafting Standard" will modify these sections according to the standard.

In the "Detailing" area we can change what is displayed in parts and assemblies; for drawings we have more options including which annotations are automatically inserted when a new drawing view is created.

In the "Units" section, select the units that we want to use in the template, number of decimal places or fractional values, angular units, length, mass, volume and force, etc. Selecting a unit system will change all the corresponding units to that system, saving us time. Selecting "Custom" will allow us to mix unit systems if so desired.

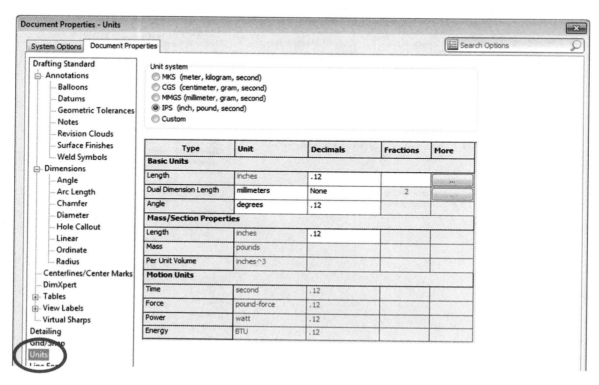

In the "Grid/Snap" section, we can define if we want to have a grid and its settings when we work in a sketch. Most users don't use the grid, but that's precisely why it's called an option. Turn it on if you like it; turn it off if you don't. It may be useful for a new user to help him/her identify when working in a sketch.

Click OK to set the new document properties to the selected options. mnother option to save with the template is the material, for this part template select the aluminum alloy 6061-T6. To save the document as a new template, go to the menu "**File, Save As**." From the "Save As Type" drop down box, select "Part Template (*.prtdot)", "Assembly Template (*.asmdot)" or "Drawing Template (*.drwdot)" (depending on the type of document we are working on.) SolidWorks will automatically change to the first folder listed under the "File Locations" list for templates; if needed, browse to the "*MySWTemplates*" folder, give it a name and click "Save." As a suggestion, give the template a name that tells you something about the options set in it, like material, standard, units, etc. or whatever works for you.

After saving the template, when we select the "**New Document**" icon and use the "**Advanced**" option, we'll see a new "Templates" tab with our new templates listed in it.

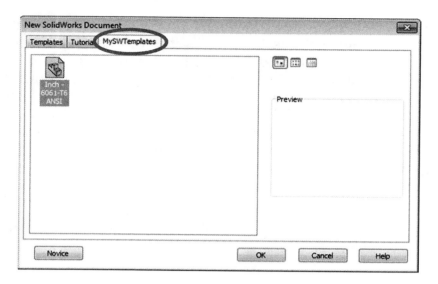

Drawing templates will include the sheet format and title block with any changes and modifications to it. If editing a drawing, select "Edit Sheet Format" from the right-mouse-click pop-up menu; change the annotations and title block to your needs. When finished modifying it, select "Edit Sheet" from the right mouse button menu and save as a drawing template. When using this template, all notes and annotations will be set.

Engine Part Features Sequence

Features sequence of selected engine parts
Crank case top

Main body	Corner Fillets	Flange	Bearing mount boss
Mirror bearing mount	Shell part	Top cut	add 0.375" offset plane inside
Add inside bosses. Use Intersecting curve	Add front reinforcement	Add rear reinforcement	Add bearing mount
Add plane for oil dipstick	Add reference sketch for dipstick	Add plane at top of reference sketch	Add dipstick extrusion
Make hole for dipstick	Add sweep cut for threaded cap	Add fillets	Add holes and threads

Engine Block

Oil Pan

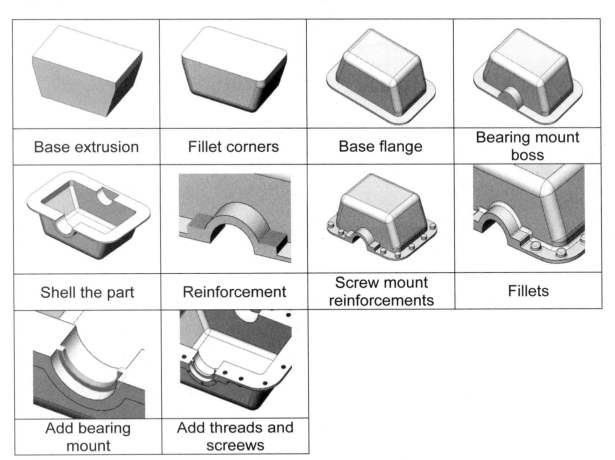

Base extrusion	Fillet corners	Base flange	Bearing mount boss
Shell the part	Reinforcement	Screw mount reinforcements	Fillets
Add bearing mount	Add threads and screews		

Piston Head

Revolved base	First cut	First bottom cut	Second bottom cut
Round inside edges	Side Cut	Groove cut	Mirror grove cut

Notes:

Index

Notes: